the Family TABLE

the Family TABLE

RECIPES AND MOMENTS FROM
A NOMADIC LIFE

JAZZ SMOLLETT-WARWELL

JURNEE SMOLLETT-BELL

JAKE SMOLLETT

JUSSIE SMOLLETT

WM
WILLIAM MORROW

An Imprint of HarperCollinsPublishers

To,

our mom, Janet, who built the family table with her own hands, nurtured us, sacrificed, and taught us to create with love in the kitchen and beyond, and whose imagination colored our lives in more ways than can be counted.

To,

our father, Joel Sr., who lives on in our hearts and who continues to watch over us from heaven above. Thank you both for giving us such unforgettable experiences through food, life, and culture that will fill us up for a lifetime.

To,

Nylah and Hunter and all the babies of the next generation, may you always be blessed with joy and a sense of wonder. May you take great interest in discovering the flavors of the world, enjoying your food with passion, and savoring every bite!

CONTENTS

INTRODUCTION

Our parents met at nineteen and twenty-three years old while working at a sweater factory in San Francisco. Mom was a sweater checker, in charge of making sure all the merchandise was properly packed and accounted for. Dad worked in the stockroom and unloaded boxes from the trucks. One day he had a co-worker pass her a note written on a piece of a cardboard box. The note said, simply, "Hi." When Mom asked who it was from, the guy gestured to Dad, who was leaning against the doorway.

They were each young and hopeful transplants from other regions. Dad, who was Jewish and of an eastern European background, grew up in Queens, New York, and Mom, who is African American, was born on Galveston Island in Texas and was raised in New Orleans. Dad had moved to California with dreams of being a boxer; Mom, with dreams of being a writer. Both come from wounded pasts, but in each other they found a youthful idealism and an "us against the world" kind of romance. A multicultural couple, they were the embodiment of the era's social justice movement, spending much of their time with civil and human rights leaders. They spent weekends leading young workers' meetings and fighting for minority and union rights. After only six weeks of dating, they moved in together, then later married. They both longed for a family and were determined to create a tribe of their own, with a goal of having ten children.

They started having children two years later. The first of the eventual six kids, Jojo, was born in the late-summer heat wave of 1977 in Queens. Mom, determined not to leave the kids with anyone else, quit working to be with us full-time, and Dad, a salt-of-the-earth, blue-collar kind of guy,

The family when there were just three out of eight! That is Jojo under a year old in the late seventies.

worked three jobs at a time while going to night school to be a data analyst. Young and idealistic but broke, they built all our furniture themselves. Trying to make a life for their young family, they would spend the next years searching for the place they would settle and call home.

We spent much of our collective childhoods exploring. Our family moved coast to coast from New York to California thirteen times, visiting countless small towns and big cities across the country. We rarely flew to destinations—getting six kids on a flight would have been both a hassle and an impossible expense—so we traveled everywhere by car, bunking up at hotels and stopping at roadside diners, small candy shops, and farmers' markets along the way. Traversing the country—first in a little Datsun with an attached U-Haul trailer and later in a long black Suburban with three rows of seats—was an adventure like no other. Being a food-minded family,

Jazz's second birthday on the side of the road, somewhere in Nebrask during a move.

our travels offered a window into different cultures and food traditions. We enjoyed chile paste in New Mexico, garlic in Gilroy, California, and clams in Maryland.

Our multicultural, nomadic family was completely normal to us. We didn't really know what other kids did—how often they moved, which holidays they celebrated, how spicy their food was, or what they ate on their matzo—if they even ate matzo.

THE FAMILY TABLE

No matter where we ended up, there were two constants in our life: big weekly family feasts and a long communal kitchen table.

Upon arriving at a new home, Mom (with Dad as her trusty assistant) would build a long kitchen table using thick wood planks she formed into a piece of butcher block, a jigsaw, bolts, and bonding materials. She would sand it smooth and finish it off with either a sugar or wine-colored varnish and a thick coat of shellac.

Another version of our mom's table! And the roasting pan is full of a homemade deep-dish pizza because Jojo is turning ten. Jurnee is looking at the camera wondering when we will eat.

Since we moved so often and the tables were very heavy, she usually re-created a new one for every new home. Mom took great care in the creation of her table, and the ritual typically lasted three days, her patience and artistry coming through as she built the perfect table for the space. We were all very proud of the table and would show it off to anyone who came to visit. It became a conversation piece among friends and was always the center of our home.

Food and food preparation were the focus of our family life and culture growing up, and we celebrated everything around that kitchen table: birthdays, Christmas, Easter, Passover, Chanukah, and any accomplishment, large or small. We often had parties, with lots of company over for dinner, but even when no one came over, the eight of us filled our large table pretty well. A multicultural family, we sometimes did things a little differently, opening our Chanukah gifts around the Christmas tree and lighting a menorah my mom had

A hiking pit stop on one of our many road trips. We made it to the top!

hand-carved out of wood, and if Easter and Passover landed on the same day, we'd celebrate them together.

Our family food life was no different: We loved eating Louisiana sausage on bagels, pickled pigs' feet from the jar with hot sauce, and gefilte fish and horseradish on matzo. Our weekly feasts featured large one-pot meals like gumbo or jambalaya, with the pot sitting center stage on a rustic coaster (made, of course, from a tree stump). There was always a baguette with olive oil and butter and a huge salad in a big wooden bowl.

The kitchen table was also where life happened. It's where we kids had our earliest lessons in how to talk loudly and skillfully enough to be heard as we engaged with the social and political issues of the day. It's where our parents would tell us there was a new baby coming. It's where they went over bills and where we did our homework. That table even saved our lives—after the 1994 earthquake in Northridge, California, we all

In front of our little green Datsun on a move across the country.

slept under it during a week of aftershocks, to protect ourselves from falling objects and debris. In a nomadic family with few constants, that table was central to our survival in more ways than one. Along with the love that bonded us together, our table sustained us, protected us, and nourished us. And as the family grew, so did the kitchen table. By the time the last kid left home, our table was eleven feet long!

Our mom was also a creative genius when it came to cooking. She had to be. With six kids, she knew how to stretch a food budget and make incredible meals out of anything we had on hand. She made pretty much everything from scratch, from fondly remembered "junk food," like doughnuts, cookies, chips, ice cream, pies, and cakes, to homemade breads, bagels, pasta sauces, and salad dressings. As family life became hectic, she became a pro at dressing up and adding flair to already-made foods, turning Top Ramen into an earthy, elevated delight (before that was even a thing). She would toss out

Jojo making homemade bread. He's so serious about it!

the packaged seasoning and add mixed mushrooms, chicken, miso paste, liquid aminos, and green onions, along with kale, spinach, or bok choy.

We may have eaten well, but we were definitely *not* raised with a spoon—silver or otherwise—handed to us. We learned early on to contribute in the kitchen, each of us starting to cook and becoming responsible for family meals before second grade. It became a friendly competition as we asked each other, "What are you making on your night to cook?" We learned to cook by necessity, but it turned into a labor of love that continues to color our culinary experiences to this day.

Jojo, our oldest brother, was a master when it came to his homemade pizza, probably because it was always his favorite food. According to our parents, he was actually weaned from breast milk at almost three years old with the best New York pizza! I, Jazz, am known for bringing out the best in my baked goods and working

Someone has to stuff the turkey on Thanksgiving!

really well with beans and legumes, since I am the self-proclaimed bean queen. Jussie specializes in curry spices and bringing sweet flavors to savory dishes. He loves to cook with various veggies that add flavor to all his dishes, but his favorite by far is peas! Jurnee is known for the creative way she dresses up traditional dishes with nontraditional ingredients. She is also queen of the carbs and can whip up the best side dishes in minutes. Jake is the all-around king of the grill and adds fiery spice and flavor to anything he cooks. He'll always be the best resource for carnivores. And Jocqui is at his best when working with pasta, since that's all he ever wants to eat.

Our food adventures weren't limited to home, either. When we were living in Queens, we'd visit a produce market called Top Tomato with our mom. It was located underneath the subway overpass and always packed. Then we'd head to the fresh fish market, because Mom was serious about getting the best quality she could find.

This was the year Passover and Easter fell on the same day. We took full advantage.

The floor would be wet and fishy from the fishmongers scaling and cleaning the fresh fish for their customers. Mom would be wearing a nursing baby in a carrier, holding a toddler's hand, and shouting her order over a crowd of patrons, with two more of us kids standing behind her. She was always on the move with us, no matter how big her tribe got. She'd pile us in the car several times a week to meet Dad for lunch if he was working the day shift or to pick him up if he had done the overnight shift.

Dad often worked the graveyard shift as a computer technician, and he'd sometimes bring one or two of us at a time to work with him on those nights. I remember him punching in with an electronic time clock when he got there and punching out when he left. I also remember the sound of those original computers as they endlessly spewed out countless lengths of green and white perforated paper. I'm not sure if we were supposed to be there or if his boss just put up with it because he knew Dad would still get his work done.

In Louisiana! Jurnee, Jake, and Jocqui made a new best friend.

I remember how cold the room was kept so that the computers didn't overheat and how bright the ceiling lights were as we pretended to sleep while Dad hustled around the room checking on those papers. For our beds, he'd push several rolling chairs together for us to sleep on, then cover us with his jacket. It was next to impossible to sleep on two rolling chairs, as they moved apart every time we moved, but we were so happy to be there with him, and his job seemed straight out of *Back to the Future*.

After the quiet of those graveyard shifts, we'd stroll out to "lunch" at Yips on Beaver Street in the Financial District, which at the time we thought was the best Chinese food around. We always ordered egg rolls and pepper steak over fried rice with lots of hot sauce, hardly able to contain the excitement of eating lunch with our dad at 10 A.M. We'd return home to Mom with leftover Chinese food, random drawings on perforated computer paper, and sore backs from napping on rolling chairs.

Happy third birthday, Jurn!

Whether at home or on the road, these exciting childhood adventures have turned into cherished memories, and as we've all moved on to the adventures of our individual lives, with busy careers, families of our own, and explorations that take us far away, we've hunted, gathered, tasted, and prepared an even wider array of cuisines from all over the world. Food has remained for each of us the way we explore and touch the world, the way we connect with others, and the best way we know to celebrate life. The food we prepare for these gatherings is a reflection of our love and our passions. It's that universal ritual of growing up and coming back home to gather with those who know us best.

We hope you enjoy creating love with these old and new family recipes and that you find magic at every kitchen table you build. Here's to wandering—and to coming home.

With love,
JAZZ

Rowdy Sunday dinners! This was the whole fam soon after Jocqui's birth in 1993. We were living in the Valley near Los Angeles.

THE SPICE OF LIFE

Since our mom loves all types of specialty food markets, we often visited spice markets, especially when we lived in Queens, where we were exposed to Jamaican and Caribbean spices as well as those from China, Italy, and India.

We loved to incorporate diverse flavors into dishes where they wouldn't usually be found. Mom used cumin on her baby back ribs, we put dill in our mac and cheese, and we always used Italian herbs in traditionally southern foods. In addition we add fresh garlic to almost everything and lots of it!

Here are the dried spices, salts, oils, and seasonings that we love. Some of them we always had on hand growing up and others we discovered later in life, but they have become staples in our recipes. This list is useful when stocking your pantry for the recipes in this book.

Basil	Olive oil
Bay leaves	Oregano
Cardamom	Paprika
Cayenne	Peppercorns
Celery salt	Pink Himalayan salt
Chile flakes	
Cinnamon	Rosemary
Coriander	Sage
Creole seasoning	Sea salt
Cumin	Sesame oil
Curry powder	Sesame seeds
Dill	Smoked paprika
Granulated garlic	Thyme
Granulated onion	Turmeric
Kosher salt	Wasabi paste
Nutmeg	White pepper

TOOLS OF THE TRADE

Mommy's reverence for cooking begins with her pots of choice, which she cares for with the dignity she might extend to a member of the family. They're her vessels of creation, and as kids we saw how she would let their individual strengths and weaknesses dictate how and when she used them. The more you work with these tools, the easier it becomes to choose the perfect one for every dish. Used correctly, pots are the ultimate partner for any cook, whether novice or expert.

The cast-iron skillet is the backbone of our kitchen, and it can be your reliable friend, too—if it isn't already. While it's excellent for stovetop cooking, the real strength of cast iron is showcased when it is transferred effortlessly from stovetop to oven. The material heats and cools slowly, making it the perfect choice for cooking casseroles, slow-cooked meats, and more. And dishes such as stews and dense breads are perfect for clay pots. Mommy often baked bread in these delicate, hand-poured vessels; she helped us understand the history and artistry that went into them.

One absolute must-have in our family is a gumbo pot. Mommy has had the same gumbo pot since 1979. Nearly every birthday in the early years, she made gumbo in this pot. It was a meal reserved for special occasions. It was a gift to enjoy the bold flavors of our family's lineage. Her gumbo pot is a symbol of our New Orleans roots.

These are the pots of our childhood, as we remember a kitchen filled with hand-me-down cast-iron skillets, handmade clay pots, and an oversize gumbo pot that will last for generations. We highly recommend adding these instruments to your kitchen's collection. We promise that you'll enjoy playing and creating with these tools! —JURNEE

HOW TO BUILD
a
Family
Table

Our mom repeated this ritual pretty much at every new home we arrived at.
Turn on the water, electricity, gas, phone, cable . . . and build a family table.
Since we would spend much of our time eating, talking, and prepping food,
the table was essential to making each new apartment (or house) into a home.
The table in this book is her most recent creation.

1. Go to the lumberyard and buy wood.

**2. Use wood glue to hold planks of wood together
and attach wood clamps to bond.**

**3. Use nuts, bolts, a drill, and a wrench
to put the legs on.**

4. Sand the table with a sander. Use goggles!

5. Varnish the table with a rag.

**6. Wait for the varnish to dry.
Put a coat of shellac over the varnish.**

7. Show it off!

SUNDAY
Suppers

JAZZ: Our parents were a bit offbeat, and our house growing up was far from perfect. The kitchen wasn't always clean, the toys weren't always in their place, and the floors were sometimes sticky. The dinner on any given night may have been made by a nine-year-old, with pots on the table doubling as serving dishes. There was probably a baby attached to our mom's breast, and the whole family was loud, rarely waiting for someone to finish a sentence before three others started speaking.

But there was a functional warmth that we wouldn't have traded for any amount of proper decorum, and on Sundays our dinner table would come especially alive. Everyone would be home, and Stevie Wonder and Bonnie Raitt records would blast in the background. The younger kids would set the table as directed by our New Orleans mother, although with her free-flowing, colorful personality, the dinnerware rarely matched. On the table sat salad dressing, a bottle of hot sauce, and a jar of jalapeños as we feasted, talking over each other about the current election or the outcome of the most recent sibling baseball game that our oldest brother, Jojo, forced us to play. There was a magic to those Sundays. They had a richness to them that would carry our family through the week—and perhaps even through a lifetime.

Stuffed Cornish Hens

JURNEE: I remember Mommy teaching me how to cook these hens when I was eight. It was the first main course she had ever tasked me with. While I was too young to carry the heavy baking dish to and from the oven (a job my oldest brother, Jojo, kindly offered to do), this became my signature dish. Mine. And I was proud of it.

At first, the recipe was very basic . . . *very*. The hens were topped with Creole seasoning, black pepper, and sliced onions, and I noticed that my brother Jake would load it up with hot sauce, which I took as a direct challenge to my skills. As I gained confidence in my cooking, I began experimenting with different flavors and methods of cooking and stuffing these delicate birds. Not to be conceited, but I have to say that this recipe has grown to perfection! Hot sauce is now optional. MAKES 2 TO 4 SERVINGS

STUFFING

One 10-ounce French baguette,
   cut into 1-inch cubes (about 11 cups)
2 tablespoons salted butter
1 tablespoon olive oil
¼ cup roughly chopped yellow onion
5 garlic cloves, minced
1 celery stalk, finely diced
⅓ cup chopped fresh basil leaves
¼ cup roughly chopped fresh oregano
¼ cup chopped fresh flat-leaf parsley
1 turkey sausage link, casing removed
2 cups low-sodium chicken stock

HENS

2 Cornish game hens (1½ to 2 pounds
   each)
8 garlic cloves
1 teaspoon sea salt
3 teaspoons dried basil
½ teaspoon crushed red pepper
1 teaspoon ground white pepper
1 teaspoon granulated onion
1 teaspoon granulated garlic
4 tablespoons (½ stick) salted butter
½ medium yellow onion, finely chopped
1 cup roughly chopped white mushrooms
   (about 3 large mushrooms)
½ cup dry white wine
¼ cup apple cider vinegar
¼ cup chopped fresh basil

PREHEAT the oven to 350°F.

TO make the stuffing, spread the baguette cubes on a rimmed baking sheet. Toast for 10 minutes, or until lightly browned. Set aside.

MELT the butter in the oil in a large saucepan or Dutch oven over high heat. Add the onion, garlic, and celery and sauté for about 2 minutes, or until translucent. Add the basil, oregano, and parsley and sauté for

15 seconds, then add the sausage and cook for 1 minute, breaking it up with a wooden spoon. Add the toasted bread and the stock, stir to combine, and cook for about 4 minutes, or until the liquid is reduced. Set aside.

TO make the hens, remove the heart, neck, gizzard, and liver and set aside or freeze for later use, either in a gravy or a dish like dirty rice.

ROUGHLY chop the garlic cloves in a food processor; you want it chunky. Add the salt, dried basil, crushed red pepper, white pepper, granulated onion, granulated garlic, and butter and blend until the mixture forms a paste.

PAT the hens dry with a paper towel. Rub the paste all over the hens, including under the skin. Place the hens breast side up in a roasting pan and surround them with the onion, mushrooms, wine, vinegar, and fresh basil. Cover the pan tightly (use foil if you don't have a lid) and roast for 45 minutes. Uncover and baste the hens with the pan juices.

SPREAD the bread mixture over the mushrooms and onions around the hens and bake for 45 minutes, or until the hens are tender. Let the hens rest for 5 minutes, then use a small spoon to stuff the hens with a little stuffing. If serving four people, cut the hens in half lengthwise. Serve with the remaining stuffing alongside.

Brown Butter Lamb Chops

JURNEE: Lamb, the other red meat. Although it's one of my favorites, it can be tricky if you underseason it. Trust me, these are certainly not underseasoned! The keys to this recipe are the rosemary marinade and the browning of the butter, so you'll need to give the meat time to absorb all the delicious flavors in the marinade, then watch your timing carefully, as you want the butter to char both sides of the meat. Butter makes everything better, and these are especially good served with mashed potatoes.

MAKES 4 SERVINGS

---

12 bone-in lamb chops (about 4 ounces each)
¼ cup extra-virgin olive oil
⅓ cup balsamic vinegar
1 teaspoon kosher salt
½ teaspoon freshly ground black pepper

8 fresh rosemary sprigs
4 tablespoons (½ stick) salted butter
12 garlic cloves, halved lengthwise
24 pearl onions (about 4 cups) or ½ larger yellow onion

PLACE the lamb chops in a gallon-size zip-top freezer bag and add the oil, vinegar, salt, pepper, and rosemary. Seal the bag and toss the chops around, making sure they are coated evenly. Marinate the lamb in the fridge for 30 to 45 minutes.

REMOVE the lamb chops from the fridge and heat a large skillet over high heat (I use cast iron, but any will do). This needs to be a quick high-heat cooking situation—you don't want the lamb chops to steam. When the skillet is nice and hot, lay the chops in the pan (you will need to work in two batches so as not to overcrowd the pan).

When you place the cold meat in the pan, the temperature of the skillet will drop, so let it rebuild heat for 1 or 2 minutes. Drop in half the butter and add half the garlic and onions. Then add half the rosemary from the marinade, saving the other half for the second batch.

COOK the chops for about 5 minutes per side for that perfect cut of pink in the middle and butter char on the outside. If you prefer your chops well done, it will take 5 to 7 minutes on each side.

TRANSFER the lamb chops and veggies to a platter and serve family-style.

North African Chicken and Spinach Stew

JAZZ: When I was seven years old, we lived in Elmhurst, Queens, surrounded by different cultures. We lived in what's called a three-family house, which is simply a brownstone separated into three apartments, one per floor. The family upstairs was Indian and the family downstairs was Chinese. Our friends in the building to the left of us were from Afghanistan and told us stories of how they escaped their nation's civil war. Our Italian friend across the street talked about his Sicilian grandmother and the desserts she made. The little Iranian girl who lived in the building to the right of us was Jussie's first crush.

Of course we all played together; there were no boundaries. Our favorite game was stickball. We played in the middle of the street and looked out for each other by yelling "car!" as a signal to clear out of the street every time we'd see a car coming. As kids, we didn't care about the differences between us; we cherished the stories we shared about our lives and the different foods we tried while at each other's houses.

This particular dish came about from a meal we had at a friend's birthday party down the street. We came home raving about it and had to try it! This is our mom's version. **MAKES 4 TO 6 SERVINGS**

---

1 whole chicken (about 2½ pounds)
3 celery stalks, roughly chopped
2 carrots, roughly chopped
1 medium onion, roughly chopped
3 bay leaves
Sea salt
10 garlic cloves
6 tablespoons (¾ stick) salted butter
½ teaspoon freshly cracked black pepper

1 cinnamon stick
10 ounces baby spinach, chopped (about 8 cups)
1 tablespoon granulated onion
1 tablespoon granulated garlic
1 tablespoon paprika
¼ teaspoon cayenne pepper
1 tablespoon dried oregano
Cooked basmati rice, for serving
Lemon wedges, for serving (optional)

PLACE the chicken in a large pot and cover it with water. Add the celery, carrot, onion, and bay leaves and season with 1 tablespoon salt. Cover and bring to a boil, then reduce the heat and simmer for 45 minutes.

REMOVE the chicken to a deep dish or bowl and let it drain. Strain the stock into a large bowl or pan and set aside. Transfer the vegetables from the strainer to a blender (remove the bay leaves), add the garlic, and puree until completely smooth. Set aside.

TO make the spinach stew, in a large saucepan over medium heat, melt 4 tablespoons of the butter. When it's bubbling slightly, add the vegetable puree. Warm it through, about 2 minutes. Season with 1 teaspoon salt, the pepper, and the cinnamon stick, then add the spinach and cook until wilted, about 2 minutes. Add 1½ cups of the reserved stock and bring to a simmer. Cook to let the flavors develop, about 15 minutes. Reduce the heat and keep warm (remove the cinnamon stick before serving).

MEANWHILE, when the chicken is cool enough to handle, pat it completely dry and break it down into 8 pieces: 2 thighs, 2 wings, and 2 breasts, then split the breasts in half. Place the chicken pieces in a large dish. Combine the granulated onion, granulated garlic, paprika, cayenne, oregano, and 1 teaspoon salt in a small bowl. Completely coat the chicken in this dry rub.

MELT the remaining 2 tablespoons butter in a large cast-iron skillet over high heat. Add the chicken pieces and sear until charred in spots, about 4 minutes. Flip and cook on the other side, 4 minutes. Remove from the heat.

SERVE the chicken with rice and a generous ladle of spinach stew. Squeeze lemon over the plate if desired.

Rustic Vegetable Ramen

JURNEE: Mommy turned standard packaged ramen noodles into an elevated earthy delight, tossing out the seasoning packet and adding fresh, colorful produce. Feel free to improvise with your favorite veggies and make this ramen your own, and when cold weather comes, grab a book and a blanket and curl up with a nice warming bowl.

MAKES 4 TO 6 LARGE SERVINGS

---

10 garlic cloves, crushed

1 large yellow onion, roughly chopped

2 carrots, roughly chopped

2 celery stalks, roughly chopped

Six 1-inch slices peeled fresh ginger

1½ tablespoons kosher salt

1 tablespoon toasted sesame oil

¼ cup liquid aminos

Head of baby bok choy, cut into ¼-inch slices

6 green onions (white and green parts), finely sliced

Handful of snow peas

One 8-ounce can sliced bamboo shoots, drained

8 fresh shiitake mushrooms

Three 3-ounce packages ramen noodles, seasoning packets discarded

Cooked chicken, pork, or seafood (optional)

4 to 6 eggs, cooked to your preference (optional)

1 jalapeño chile, thinly sliced (optional)

Sriracha, to taste (optional)

COMBINE 8 cups water, the garlic, onion, carrots, celery, and ginger in a large Dutch oven or heavy-bottomed stockpot. Bring to a boil, then add the salt, oil, and liquid aminos. Reduce the heat to medium and let the veggies simmer for 25 to 30 minutes, to develop a well-flavored stock. Remove the stock from the heat and strain it into a large saucepan. Discard the cooked vegetables. (You can make the stock ahead of time and refrigerate for up to 3 days or freeze for up to 6 months.)

RETURN the stock to medium heat and bring it to a simmer. Add the bok choy, green onions, snow peas, bamboo shoots, mushrooms, and ramen. When the noodles are soft, about 3 minutes, remove from the heat and serve.

YOU can add cooked chicken, pork, or seafood to this easy recipe as well—just throw it in with the ramen to heat through. I top mine with a soft-boiled egg, sliced jalapeño, and sriracha for that extra added kick! Enjoy!

Mom's Pot Roast

JAZZ: My earliest memories are of my mom in the kitchen on a Sunday with tiny bells on her flowing skirt making dishes like this pot roast. For as long as I can remember, she has been a romantic. She lives in a dreamy world of magic and possibility. Her imagination is wild, and she is uncontained in her expression. Watching her cook and create was one of the great joys of my childhood. I love this simple and beautiful roast because it is infused with a kind of romantic magic all its own. It's also delicious!

MAKES 8 SERVINGS

2 tablespoons canola oil
2½ pounds tri-tip roast or rump roast
2 teaspoons sea salt
1 teaspoon ground white pepper
8 fresh thyme sprigs
12 garlic cloves, minced
½ yellow onion, chopped
Bunch of carrots, multicolored
    preferred, sliced into ½-inch rounds
    (about 3 cups)
2 tablespoons chopped fresh oregano

2 tablespoons chopped fresh flat-leaf
    parsley
2 tablespoons chopped fresh basil
10 baby bella mushrooms, stemmed and
    quartered
2 tablespoons unbleached all-purpose flour
½ cup dry white wine
2 cups low-sodium beef stock
4 baby Yukon Gold potatoes, scrubbed
    and quartered
4 baby red potatoes, scrubbed and
    quartered

HEAT the oil in a deep cast-iron pot or Dutch oven over high heat for 1 to 2 minutes, until sizzling. Season the beef with 1 teaspoon of the salt and ½ teaspoon of the white pepper. Sear the beef on one side for 6 minutes, until brown, then add the thyme to the pot and sear the other side for 4 to 5 more minutes, until brown. Remove the meat and thyme from the pot and set aside.

WITH the pot still over high heat, add the garlic, onion, carrot, and herbs and sweat the aromatics for about 3 minutes, stirring frequently. Add the mushrooms and sauté for 3 minutes. Sprinkle the flour in and stir to coat the mushrooms and veggies. Add the wine and stock, scraping the bottom of the pot to loosen all the caramelized bits. Return the beef and all its resting juices to the pot and lay the thyme on top. Season with the remaining salt and white pepper. Bring the mixture to a boil, then reduce the heat to a simmer and cover.

COOK the pot roast over low heat for about 1 hour, then flip the meat, cover, and cook for another hour. Add the potatoes, give the mixture a stir, cover, and cook for 30 minutes, or until completely tender.

REMOVE the beef to a cutting board and slice against the grain into ½-inch pieces. Serve with the mushrooms and vegetables.

Chicken Taco Lasagna

JAKE: Chicken taco lasagna falls somewhere between a juicy burrito and an enchilada, but it's layered lasagna-style. Mexican food was big in our household when we lived in Southern California because it was easy to find really great spices and fresh ingredients at the awesome Mexican grocery stores near our neighborhood. This is a dish that the entire family will love, and it goes a long way.

MAKES 6 TO 8 SERVINGS

1 tablespoon vegetable oil
½ yellow onion, finely chopped
1 jalapeño chile, seeded and finely diced
2 pounds ground chicken
1 tablespoon chili powder
1½ teaspoons ground cumin
1½ teaspoons sea salt
2 handfuls of fresh cilantro, chopped
One 15-ounce can low-sodium black
     beans, drained and rinsed
Two 14.5-ounce cans no-salt-added
     diced tomatoes, 1 can drained of juice
4 green onions, thinly sliced

3 cups shredded Monterey Jack
     (about 12 ounces)
3 cups shredded sharp white Cheddar
     (about 12 ounces)
1 cup shredded pepper Jack
     (about 4 ounces)
Three 12-inch flour tortillas
1 cup sour cream
2 tablespoons Mexican hot sauce (I like
     Valentina)
1 vine-ripened tomato, thinly sliced
1 Hass avocado, pitted, peeled, and
     thinly sliced

PREHEAT the oven to 375°F.

HEAT the oil in a large heavy-bottomed pot over medium-high heat, add the onion and jalapeño, and sauté until soft, 2 minutes. Add the chicken and season it with the chili powder, cumin, salt, and half the cilantro. Cook the chicken until it's browned and cooked through, about 5 minutes, breaking it up with a wooden spoon. Add the beans and diced tomatoes and bring the mixture to a simmer. Cook for 10 minutes, remove the pan from the heat, and add half the green onions (you want them to keep a nice crunch).

MIX together the cheeses in a large bowl and set aside.

PLACE the tortillas on a baking sheet and bake for 3 to 5 minutes to get them a little crunchy. Remove from the oven and build the lasagna. Layer one tortilla at the bottom of a cast-iron pan then top with one third of the chicken mixture, then one third of the cheese blend, and top with a second tortilla. Add half the remaining chicken mixture, then half the remaining cheese, and top with the remaining tortilla. Spread the remaining chicken mixture and cheese on

top. Bake for 20 minutes, or until the cheese is browned and bubbly. Set aside to cool slightly before serving.

WHISK together the sour cream and hot sauce in a small bowl. Top the lasagna with tomato and avocado slices, the remaining green onions and cilantro, and the spicy sour cream.

Tangerine Chicken Strips

JAKE: New York–style Chinese food can't be beat, and as a kid living in New York, I would run into the delis and make a beeline for the orange chicken at the hot-food bar. This is my take on orange chicken, with tangerine juice making a tangy sauce that goes perfectly over steamed rice or veggies.

MAKES 2 TO 4 MAIN OR 6 TO 8 APPETIZER SERVINGS

SAUCE

4 or 5 medium tangerines
3½ tablespoons low-sodium soy sauce
1 tablespoon toasted sesame oil
1 heaping tablespoon finely grated
    peeled fresh ginger
4 garlic cloves, minced
2 tablespoons unsweetened applesauce
1 tablespoon sriracha
1 tablespoon honey
1½ teaspoons unbleached all-purpose
    flour

CHICKEN

Vegetable oil, for frying
1 pound chicken tenders
1 teaspoon sea salt
1 cup unbleached all-purpose flour
Sliced green onions, for serving
Cooked white basmati rice, for serving
    (optional)

TO make the sauce, peel the tangerine rinds into thin slices with a vegetable peeler and set aside. Juice the tangerines into a measuring cup; you should have about 1 cup.

COMBINE the tangerine juice, soy sauce, sesame oil, ginger, garlic, applesauce, sriracha, and honey in a large saucepan and cook over medium-high heat until smooth, flavorful, and thick, about 12 minutes. Strain out the garlic and ginger tidbits, then return the sauce to the pan and add the flour. Cook over medium-high heat for 8 to 10 minutes, until the sauce is thick enough to coat the back of a spoon. Set aside off the heat while you fry the chicken.

TO make the chicken, heat the vegetable oil in a large cast-iron skillet or heavy-bottomed frying pan over high heat until very hot. (Sprinkle a little flour in the oil and if it sizzles, the oil is ready.)

LINE a plate with paper towels and set aside. Place the chicken, salt, and flour in a large bowl and toss to coat the chicken completely in flour. Shake off any excess flour. Working in batches so as not to overcrowd the skillet, fry the chicken for 5 to 7 minutes per side, until golden brown. As you finish, place the chicken on the lined plate to absorb the oil.

TRANSFER the fried chicken to the delicious tangerine sauce, coating the pieces thoroughly. Top with green onions and the reserved tangerine peels. Rice is an awesome accompaniment, too!

Hearty Black Bean Chili

JAKE: Nothing beats a bowl of black bean chili—whether it's cold out and you feel like a bowl with corn bread or it's warm out and you use it to top a nice chili dog, it's always a home run. And it's that one-pot meal for which I usually have all the ingredients on hand to make a nice big batch. As long as you have ground meat, tomatoes, garlic, onions, black beans, and seasonings, you're good to go.

MAKES 6 TO 8 SERVINGS

3 tablespoons olive oil

12 garlic cloves, minced

½ large jalapeño chile, seeded and minced

¼ yellow bell pepper, cored, seeded, and cut into small dice

¼ red bell pepper, cored, seeded, and cut into small dice

¼ large onion, cut into small dice

2 pounds ground turkey

2½ teaspoons salt

3 tablespoons chili powder

2 tablespoons ground cumin

1 tablespoon dried basil

1 tablespoon dried oregano

10 Roma tomatoes, cut into medium dice

Two 15-ounce cans low-sodium black beans, drained and rinsed

2 tablespoons Louisiana hot sauce

Bunch of green onions, thinly sliced, for serving

Sour cream, for serving

2 limes, cut into wedges, for serving

HEAT the oil in a large stockpot or Dutch oven over high heat. Add the garlic, jalapeño, bell peppers, and onion and sweat, stirring occasionally, for 2 minutes. Add the turkey, salt, chili powder, cumin, basil, and oregano and cook until the turkey is cooked through, about 10 minutes, breaking it up with a wooden spoon. Add the tomatoes and stir. Reduce the heat to low, cover, and cook for 25 minutes to let the flavors marry, stirring occasionally. Add the beans, stir, and cook until warmed through. Stir in the hot sauce.

SERVE with green onions, sour cream, and lime wedges.

Lemon Fried Trout

JAKE: Fried trout makes my world go round—it sets my world on its side! When I was a kid, I would wait at the table with my plate and a bottle of Louisiana hot sauce until my mom was done frying her trout. Something about the lemony batter, the freshly fried golden brown crunch, and the buttery fish makes me melt.

MAKES 4 SERVINGS

TROUT

4 rainbow trout fillets (about 4 ounces each)
Sea salt
1 teaspoon cayenne pepper
½ cup fine-ground cornmeal
2 tablespoons unbleached all-purpose flour
1 tablespoon dried basil
1 tablespoon granulated garlic
1 tablespoon granulated onion
½ tablespoon dried oregano

1 teaspoon paprika
2 lemons
1 large egg
Vegetable oil, for frying
Lemon wedges, for serving (optional)

TARTAR SAUCE

½ cup mayonnaise
2 heaping teaspoons dill relish
2 teaspoons fresh lemon juice
¼ teaspoon sea salt

TO make the trout, place the fillets on top of paper towels to soak up any excess liquid. Season with salt to taste and the cayenne.

COMBINE the cornmeal, flour, 2 teaspoons salt, basil, granulated garlic, granulated onion, oregano, and paprika in a small bowl. Zest and juice the lemons and set aside the zest. Whisk together the egg and lemon juice in a medium bowl. Dredge a trout fillet in the egg mixture, then in the flour mixture, and set it aside on a plate. Repeat with the rest of the fillets.

LINE a plate with paper towels and set aside. Heat the oil in a large cast-iron skillet or heavy-bottomed frying pan over high heat until very hot. (Sprinkle a little of the dry spice mix in the oil and if it sizzles, the oil is ready.) Add 2 fillets to the pan skin side up and pan-fry for 1 minute, until golden. Gently flip the fillets with a fish or pancake spatula and fry for another 45 seconds, then remove them to the lined plate. Reheat the oil for 1 minute and repeat to cook the remaining fillets. Sprinkle the fillets with the reserved lemon zest.

TO make the tartar sauce, whisk together the mayonnaise, relish, lemon juice, and salt in a small bowl. Serve the fish with lemon wedges, if desired, and the sauce on the side.

Take some time to set the right tone for your Sunday party.

Stuffed Bell Peppers

JAKE: Easy to make, beautiful to serve, and perfect for dinner when you want something hearty that won't leave you feeling . . . stuffed. These peppers pair well with Butter Lettuce Apple Crisp Salad (page 114).

MAKES 8 SERVINGS (½ PEPPER PER SERVING)

---

1 tablespoon extra-virgin olive oil
5 garlic cloves, minced
½ yellow onion, finely diced
½ jalapeño chile, seeded and finely diced
Handful of fresh basil, chopped
1 tablespoon chopped fresh oregano
2 tablespoons chopped fresh flat-leaf
    parsley

½ cup diced pancetta (about 4 ounces)
1 pound ground chicken
1 teaspoon granulated garlic
2 teaspoons sea salt
4 baby bella mushrooms, finely chopped
8 Roma tomatoes, cut into small dice
4 red bell peppers, halved vertically,
    cored, and seeded

PREHEAT the oven to 375°F.

HEAT the oil in a large sauté pan over medium-high heat. Add the garlic, onion, jalapeño, 2 tablespoons of the basil, and the oregano and parsley and sauté until the veggies are soft, about 4 minutes. Remove the veggies to a bowl.

ADD the pancetta to the pan and cook over medium heat until it's crispy, about 10 minutes. Add the chicken, season with the granulated garlic and salt, and cook until the chicken is browned and cooked through, about 8 minutes, breaking it up so that it cooks evenly. Add the mushrooms, tomatoes, and cooked veggies and simmer until the tomatoes are soft and broken down, about 8 minutes.

PLACE the bell pepper halves on a rimmed baking sheet and divide the stuffing among them. Bake for 40 to 45 minutes, until the peppers are soft. Garnish with the remaining basil.

Everything Pan Pizza

JUSSIE: Our oldest brother, Jojo, has always been the pizza king in our family. It's one of the things we kind of leave alone, because his is perfect. Then one time a few years ago I visited New York City and stayed with our godsister, Jasmin. One day I asked her kids, Naomi, Fiona, and Ethan, what they wanted me to cook (I always say I can cook anything). When they said pizza, I went off—no one had ever asked me to make pizza before. It was my time to shine! So I went to the store and got every single thing I would ever dream of putting on a pizza, thus birthing the greatest pizza known to human history. Sorry, Jojo.

MAKES 6 TO 8 SERVINGS

TOPPING

12 ounces thick-cut bacon, sliced into ½-inch strips (see Note)

1 pound hot Italian turkey sausage links, casings removed

½ red bell pepper, seeded, cored, and cut into small dice

½ green bell pepper, seeded, cored, and cut into small dice

½ yellow bell pepper, seeded, cored, and cut into small dice

1 jalapeño chile, seeded and finely diced

6 garlic cloves, thinly sliced

¼ large yellow onion, cut into small dice

¼ cup chopped fresh basil

3 tablespoons chopped fresh oregano

2 cups chopped baby spinach

1½ cups grated mozzarella (about 6 ounces)

Note: Bacon is easier to cut when cold.

SAUCE

1 tablespoon olive oil

2 garlic cloves, minced

1 tablespoon dried basil

One 6-ounce can tomato paste

1 teaspoon dark brown sugar

¼ teaspoon sea salt

CRUST

¾ cup warm (110°F to 115°F) water

2 teaspoons brown sugar

One ¼-ounce package active dry yeast (about 2¼ teaspoons)

2 tablespoons olive oil, plus more for greasing

1 teaspoon sea salt

2 cups unbleached all-purpose flour, plus more for rolling out the dough

1 teaspoon granulated onion

1 teaspoon granulated garlic

1 teaspoon crushed red pepper

LINE a plate with paper towels and set aside. To make the topping, arrange the bacon in a large cast-iron skillet or heavy-bottomed frying pan over high heat and cook until crispy, 3 to 4 minutes on each side. Remove the bacon to the lined plate to absorb the excess oil. Reserve 1 tablespoon of the bacon grease in the skillet. Return the skillet to high heat, add the sausage, and cook it until it is browned and cooked through, about 5 minutes, breaking it up with a wooden spoon. Add the bell peppers, jalapeño, garlic, onion, basil, and oregano and cook, stirring often, until soft, 3 minutes. Return the bacon to the skillet and cook, stirring, another minute to marry all the flavors. Remove the skillet from the heat and stir in the spinach. The residual heat will wilt the greens. Set aside.

TO make the sauce, heat the oil in a small saucepan over medium heat. Add the garlic and basil and sweat, about 1 minute. Add the tomato paste, fill the empty can with water, and pour the water into the pan. Add the brown sugar and salt, mix to combine, and remove from the heat. Set aside and let the residual heat bring the flavors together.

TO make the crust, preheat the oven to 200°F.

POUR the water into a large bowl. Stir in the brown sugar and sprinkle the yeast over the water. Let the yeast bloom in a warm spot for 5 minutes, or until it is foamy and smooth. Add the oil, salt, and flour. Whisk slowly until the dough comes together; you may need to get in there with your hands. Work the dough until smooth.

OIL a large glass bowl and transfer the dough to it. Open the oven, place the bowl on the open oven door, and let it rise for 1 hour with the oven on, or until doubled in size.

WHEN the dough is ready, increase the oven temperature to 500°F. Flour a clean work surface and your hands. Pull the dough from the bowl onto the surface and gently knead it, folding it in on itself, for about 1 minute, until smooth. Flour a rolling pin (or wine bottle!) and roll the dough into a 17-inch rectangle that's about ⅛ inch thick.

DUST an 11 × 17-inch rimmed baking sheet evenly with the granulated onion, granulated garlic, and crushed red pepper. Transfer the crust to the baking sheet and gently stretch the dough to the edges, spreading it out to make it even. Top the dough evenly with the tomato sauce, bacon-sausage topping, and mozzarella.

BAKE until the crust is golden and the cheese has melted, 8 to 10 minutes. Cut into wedges and serve immediately!

Slow-Cooked Miso Short Ribs

JURNEE: I'm a huge fan of savory and sweet. With apricot preserves as a sweetener and savory red miso paste, this short rib recipe perfectly delivers a one-two punch, balancing the flavors beautifully. Short ribs cooked in a slow cooker take some time, but they'll have an extremely tender texture and you just throw in all the ingredients and leave it. Many people shy away from this type of rib because making sure it's tender and not rubbery can be tricky, but that's not a problem here. Warning—serve yourself first! These ribs are guaranteed to disappear quickly.

MAKES 6 TO 8 SERVINGS

6 pounds bone-in short ribs
1½ tablespoons kosher salt
1½ teaspoons crushed red pepper
3 tablespoons toasted sesame oil
1 large onion, diced
10 garlic cloves, crushed
1 leek (white part only), quartered
    lengthwise and thoroughly rinsed
¾ cup dry sherry
2 cups low-sodium beef stock
¼ cup liquid aminos
¼ cup red miso paste

2 tablespoons mirin
2 tablespoons rice vinegar
2 tablespoons apricot preserves
1½ tablespoons brown sugar
2 tablespoons minced peeled fresh
    ginger
¼ cup cornstarch
Cooked white rice, for serving
Roughly chopped green onions
    (optional)

SPECIAL EQUIPMENT: 4- to 6-quart slow
    cooker

SEASON the short ribs all over with the salt and crushed red pepper. Heat the oil in a large heavy-bottomed pan over high heat. Working in batches so as not to overcrowd the pan, cook the short ribs until browned, 3 minutes per side, then remove them to a large plate. Drain all but 2 tablespoons of the pan grease.

PLACE the pan over medium-high heat, add the onion, garlic, and leek and sauté for 3 to 4 minutes, until soft. Add the sherry and deglaze the pan, scraping up any beef bits stuck to the bottom. Transfer the onion mixture to a slow cooker, then add the stock, liquid aminos, miso, mirin,

vinegar, preserves, brown sugar, ginger, and cornstarch. Whisk, making sure the cornstarch is free of lumps. Nestle the short ribs into the liquid and pour in any juices from the plate.

COVER the slow cooker and cook on high until the meat is knife tender and falls off the bone, 4 to 6 hours, depending on your slow cooker. Let the meat and sauce cool slightly, then skim off and discard as much fat as possible.

SERVE the short ribs with white rice and, if desired, garnish with chopped green onions.

Dad's Cuban Picadillo

JAZZ: Our father went away to camp when he was seven, and he told us camp stories often for the rest of his life. He'd tell us about how he learned to swim from one of the counselors, how he loved hiking and exploring the wilderness, and how he met his best friend, Zach, who would later become our godfather. After Dad passed away three years ago, I was reading some of his letters home from camp. He talked about Zach, what he was doing at camp, and the meal he longed for, *picadillo*. This is a traditional dish in many parts of Latin America, but he grew up eating the Cuban version. Before our grandparents were married, they were part of a progressive group, and a friend from the group introduced them to this meal. This quick, foolproof dish was Dad's favorite to cook when we were kids. It was always delicious served over white rice and topped with fresh black pepper! MAKES 8 TO 10 SERVINGS

1 tablespoon olive oil
2 yellow onions, cut into medium dice
2 green bell peppers, cut into medium dice
2 pounds ground beef
½ teaspoon ground white pepper
2 teaspoons granulated onion
2 teaspoons granulated garlic

One 21-ounce jar pimento-stuffed Manzanilla olives
Two 3.5-ounce jars capers and juice
Two 28-ounce cans no-salt-added whole peeled tomatoes, 1 can drained of juice
Cooked jasmine rice, for serving
Freshly cracked black pepper

HEAT the oil in a large saucepan over medium-high heat, add the onion and bell pepper, and sauté until soft, about 4 minutes. Add the beef and season with the white pepper, granulated onion, and granulated garlic. Stir and let the mixture cook through, about 6 minutes, breaking up the meat with a wooden spoon.

ADD 2 cups of the olives, all the olive juice in the jar, the caper juice from both jars, and 1½ jars' worth of capers. Add the tomatoes and use a wooden spoon to crush them. You may save the remaining olives and capers in the freezer in an airtight container without the brine for later use in a pasta dish or salad. They should keep for 6 months.

INCREASE the heat to high and bring the mixture to a boil, then reduce the heat to low, cover the pan, and simmer until the tomatoes and olives break down, 90 minutes, stirring occasionally.

SERVE the *picadillo* with jasmine rice and top with cracked black pepper.

Teriyaki Salmon

JAZZ: We ate a lot of salmon growing up, especially once the family became very large and we started shopping at bulk grocery stores. For some reason, they always sell large salmon fillets at amazing prices. Salmon is a great fish because it's low in mercury and has a wonderfully delicate flavor. This is the perfect dish to pair with the our Garlic-Mushroom Quinoa (page 147)!   MAKES 8 TO 10 SERVINGS

TERIYAKI SAUCE

1 cup low-sodium soy sauce

1 cup rice wine vinegar

2 tablespoons toasted sesame oil

¼ cup plus 2 tablespoons honey

¼ cup unpacked light brown sugar

12 garlic cloves, minced

2 tablespoons minced peeled fresh ginger

2 tablespoons cornstarch

2 tablespoons toasted sesame seeds

4 green onions (white and light green parts), chopped, plus more for garnish (optional)

SALMON

4 heads of baby bok choy, leaves separated

1 small eggplant, cut into 1-inch dice

8 ounces cremini mushrooms, cut into ¼-inch slices

One 2-pound whole salmon fillet, skin removed

Cooked white rice, for serving

PREHEAT the oven to 400°F.

TO make the sauce, whisk together the sauce ingredients in a medium saucepan over medium heat. Cook until thickened, about 6 minutes, whisking often to make sure the cornstarch is lump-free. Remove from the heat and set aside.

TO make the salmon, arrange the bok choy, eggplant, and mushrooms in a deep 9 × 13-inch baking dish and lay the salmon on top. Make shallow diagonal slices into the salmon that are about 2 inches apart and 2 inches long. Pour the sauce over the salmon, letting it get into the slices to help flavor the fish. Bake until the salmon is opaque all the way through, 20 minutes, or to your desired doneness.

SERVE with white rice and, if desired, garnish with more green onions.

The bean (and legume) queen can't be bothered while creating her magic.

Easy Green Lentil Stew

JAZZ: Whenever I've been eating a lot of meat, sugar, cheese, and chocolate and start to crave something lighter, I often go for lentils, which my mom taught me to make. These lentils are great because they combine so many different flavors and veggies that they satisfy the appetite while still keeping it pretty light. If I'm feeling up to eating more butter, fat, and sugar, I'll pair these lentils with our yummy Jalapeño-Bacon-Cheddar Corn Bread (page 128). Just saying.

MAKES 6 TO 8 SERVINGS, WITH LEFTOVERS

2 cups green lentils, sorted and rinsed
3 carrots, halved lengthwise and cut into
    ¼-inch slices
2 celery stalks, halved lengthwise and
    cut into ¼-inch slices
1 shallot, cut into small dice

5 garlic cloves, minced
1½ teaspoons sea salt
1 tablespoon ground cumin
3 cups loosely packed baby spinach
Lime wedges, for serving (optional)

PLACE the lentils in a large stockpot and cover with 7 cups water. Bring to a boil, then reduce the heat, cover, and simmer until tender, about 20 minutes. Add the carrots, celery, shallot, and garlic and cover. Cook until the vegetables are tender, about 30 minutes. Add the salt, cumin, and spinach and cook for 5 minutes, until the leaves are wilted. Serve with lime wedges, if desired.

Spicy Fish Curry Soup

JUSSIE: It doesn't matter whether it's a hot Southern California day or a freezing Chicago night, this soupy stew is one of my favorite dishes. It feels like a little bit of the islands, a little bit of Asia, and a little bit of New Orleans all rolled into one.

MAKES 4 TO 6 SERVINGS

2 tablespoons extra-virgin olive oil
12 garlic cloves, chopped
3 shallots, finely chopped
1 cup roughly chopped fresh flat-leaf
  parsley
4 teaspoons yellow curry powder
¼ teaspoon cayenne pepper
½ teaspoon crushed red pepper
¼ teaspoon cracked black pepper
1 teaspoon granulated onion

¼ teaspoon dried oregano
5 bay leaves
2 teaspoons sea salt
2 teaspoons sugar
2 cups frozen peas
1 pound whiting (or cod) fillet, skin
  removed, cut into 1½-inch squares
Cooked basmati rice, for serving
  (optional)

HEAT the oil in a large saucepan or Dutch oven over medium-high heat. Add the garlic, shallots, and parsley and sauté until the shallots are translucent, about 2 minutes. Add the curry powder, cayenne, crushed red pepper, black pepper, granulated onion, oregano, bay leaves, salt, and sugar and stir well to coat the aromatics. Cook for about 1 minute, stirring, to toast the spices.

ADD 4 cups water and bring the mixture to a boil. Reduce the heat to low and simmer, covered, for 25 to 30 minutes. Add the peas and cook until heated through, about 4 minutes.

INCREASE the heat to high and bring the soup to a boil again. Drop in the fish, cover, and cook until the fish turns opaque and is cooked through, 5 to 7 minutes. Do not stir—the fish will break up.

REMOVE from the heat and, if desired, serve over basmati rice. So good!

Tomato Potato Turkey Meat Loaf

JAZZ: This meat loaf is incredibly tender, and it doesn't even use bread crumbs; ours includes tomato paste and a ton of herbs and spices. Growing up, I thought everyone topped their meat loaf with mashed potatoes, but three decades later, I found out we were a strange family and that no one else really did that. It's now a goal of mine for everyone to start putting potatoes over their meat loaf and discover how delicious it is! I guess it's kind of like a shepherd's pie meat loaf!? Works for me.

Love y'all!

MASHED POTATOES
1½ pounds baby red potatoes, scrubbed
½ cup whole milk
4 tablespoons (½ stick) salted butter
½ teaspoon sea salt

MEAT LOAF
3 pounds ground turkey
1 cup tomato paste
1 tablespoon sea salt
2 tablespoons olive oil
1 small red onion, finely diced
14 garlic cloves, minced

1 small yellow bell pepper, cored, seeded, and finely diced
2 tablespoons dried thyme
2 tablespoons dried basil
2 tablespoons dried oregano

TOMATO SAUCE
One 6-ounce can tomato paste
½ tablespoon olive oil
¼ teaspoon granulated garlic
¼ teaspoon sea salt

SPECIAL EQUIPMENT: large roasting pan with a lid or 9 × 13-inch casserole dish

---

PREHEAT the oven to 375°F.

PLACE the potatoes in a medium saucepan and cover with water. Bring to a boil, then reduce the heat and simmer until the potatoes are knife tender, 40 minutes. Drain the potatoes and return them to the hot pan. While the potatoes are still warm, add the milk, butter, and salt. Use a potato masher to mash the mixture until completely smooth. Set aside.

WHILE the potatoes are cooking, make the meat loaf mixture. Place the turkey, tomato paste, and salt in a large bowl. Heat the oil in a medium skillet over medium-high heat. Add the onion, garlic, bell pepper, and herbs and cook until the vegetables have softened, 5 to 6 minutes. Transfer the mixture to the ground turkey bowl. Using a spatula, stir the mixture thoroughly so all the ingredients are evenly distributed through the ground meat.

TRANSFER the meat loaf mixture to the roasting pan and form it into an even log. Cover with a lid. (If using a casserole dish, cover with foil.) Bake the meat loaf for 40 minutes.

UNCOVER the pan (don't be alarmed by the amount of juice—it will make the meat loaf nice and tender). Using a spatula, frost the meat loaf with the mashed potatoes, completely covering the top and sides of the loaf. Return the pan to the oven (uncovered) and bake until the potatoes have slightly set and feel tacky, about 15 minutes. Remove from the oven and set aside.

TO make the sauce, combine the tomato paste, oil, granulated garlic, and salt in a medium bowl. Fill the empty tomato paste can with water, add it to the mixture, and stir until incorporated.

SPREAD the tomato sauce evenly all over the potatoes, completely covering every inch. Bake, uncovered, until the tomato sauce sets and looks almost like red cake frosting, 20 minutes.

SLICE and serve immediately.

PASTA
Night

JAZZ: Pasta . . . pasta . . . *pasta!*

Why is pasta night so much fun? Maybe it's the aroma that fills the air from the garlic, tomatoes, olive oil, and basil. Maybe it's the texture of the pasta itself or the fact that cheese is almost always involved. As kids, pasta was the go-to meal when we were asked what we wanted for dinner. Something about pasta night feels like a feast, a celebration all on its own.

Italian food was a big influence on our New Yorker dad, and his favorite dish to make was spaghetti and meatballs. Mom has always had a knack for using fresh or dried Italian herbs and finding the ripest tomatoes to make the best savory sauce from scratch. Our pasta nights would involve card games like war, spit, or Uno and a tiny taste of whatever red wine was going in the sauce. Hmmm, maybe that's why we liked pasta night so much!

These are some of our favorite family pasta dishes. We think pasta should always be served family-style in a big bowl in the center of the table, along with a Caesar salad and slices of baguette. Oh, and wine, of course!

Homemade Linguine

JAKE: I went to Italy for the first time a few years ago and took pasta-making classes in Naples and Positano. I learned how to make fresh pasta right from the source, and it was one of the best experiences of my life.

MAKES 4 TO 6 SERVINGS

2 cups unbleached all-purpose flour, plus more for rolling out the dough
2 eggs
4 large egg yolks
⅓ cup finely minced fresh tarragon

Sauce of your choice, such as the one for Linguine Vongole (page 48) or Lamb Bolognese (page 44), warmed

SPECIAL EQUIPMENT: pasta roller, pasta cutter

MOUND the flour on a clean work surface. Using your fingers, make a well in the center of the mound. Pour the eggs and egg yolks into the well; add the tarragon and 1 tablespoon water. Using a fork, whisk together the eggs and yolks while incorporating the flour from the inside of the mound, working outward until the flour and eggs are combined. With the palms of your hands, knead the dough. If the dough seems dry and shaggy, dampen your hands with water and knead until the dough is moist but not wet. If it feels wet, add flour, 1 teaspoon at a time.

KNEAD the dough until smooth and elastic, about 10 minutes. Wrap the dough in plastic wrap and let it rest at room temperature for 30 minutes.

CUT the dough into equal quarters and roll each into a small, thick log about 17 inches long. Lightly flour your surface. Use your hands or a rolling pin to flatten the dough logs to about ⅛ inch thick. Feed one piece of dough through a pasta roller set to the widest setting. Fold the dough into thirds lengthwise and continue to roll, adjusting the setting each time to achieve the desired thickness. Cover with a thin towel and repeat with the remaining dough logs. Cut the sheets into the preferred noodle length.

SWITCH the pasta roller to a linguine cutter and feed each sheet through the cutter. Flour the noodles and gently separate them, or hang them on a rack to dry to prevent sticking. Repeat with all the pasta sheets. (If you won't be cooking all the pasta noodles at once, you can store the noodles in the fridge for up to 2 days. Place the noodles on a baking tray that has been lightly dusted with flour and let dry out for 2 to 3 minutes. It's best if you form the noodles into small nests and wrap in plastic to save for later.)

BRING a large pot of water to a boil, add the pasta, and cook until al dente, about 3 minutes. Remove the pasta and transfer to the pan with the warm sauce. Turn off the heat and gently stir to coat the noodles. Serve hot.

Lamb Bolognese

Rumor has it that I was brought home from the hospital in Dad's taxi cab, and that for the first few months I slept in a makeshift bassinet made from a dresser drawer. Apparently, that temporary situation ended when my parents built my crib, which was connected to my older brother Jojo's bed. Rumor also has it that pasta with meat sauce was my absolute favorite food as a toddler. I know the latter rumor to be true, since I am still always in the mood for a good bowl of pasta for dinner.

This Bolognese is no joke! I love a good Bolognese, and this one is about as good as they come.

MAKES 6 TO 8 SERVINGS

½ cup cubed pancetta (about 4 ounces)
1 tablespoon olive oil
½ medium yellow onion, finely minced
8 garlic cloves, minced
1 carrot, cut into small dice
½ cup chopped fresh basil, plus more for garnish
¼ cup minced fresh flat-leaf parsley
2 hot Italian turkey sausage links, casings removed
1 pound ground lamb
1½ teaspoons sea salt
½ teaspoon crushed red pepper

¼ teaspoon dried oregano
½ teaspoon freshly cracked black pepper
½ teaspoon brown sugar
⅓ cup dry red wine
Three 12-ounce cans no-salt-added diced tomatoes
No-sodium chicken stock, beef stock, or water, as needed
1 pound casarecce or other short and/ or twisted pasta, such as gemelli or penne
½ cup grated Parmesan

HEAT a large pot or Dutch oven over medium heat. Add the pancetta and cook it to a brown, crispy texture, about 10 minutes, stirring frequently. Add the oil, onion, garlic, carrot, basil, and parsley and sauté until soft, about 4 minutes. Add the sausage and the lamb and cook it until it's browned, about 5 minutes, breaking it up with a wooden spoon. Mix in the salt, crushed red pepper, oregano, pepper, and sugar. Add the wine, stir, and deglaze the pan, scraping up any bits stuck to the bottom. Cook for about 1 minute. Add the canned tomatoes, reduce the heat to low, and cook uncovered for 1 hour. The tomatoes will break down fully and the sauce will become rich and thick. Stir in a little stock if it gets too dry.

BRING a large pot of water to a boil, add the pasta, and cook to your preferred doneness, stirring occasionally. Drain and set aside.

ADD the pasta to the pot and gently mix to coat it with sauce. Top with Parmesan, garnish with basil, and serve immediately. You can make ahead and freeze the sauce in an airtight container for up to 3 months.

Goat Cheese Pesto Pasta

JAZZ: Right after college, while interning at an off-Broadway theater in New York City, I started working at a French restaurant in SoHo. I loved the staff meals there. An hour and a half before we opened for dinner, we'd push several tables together to create a long communal table at the center of the restaurant. We'd all set the table and eat a delicious meal prepared for us off the menu for that evening. We'd sit around the table and laugh, banter back and forth, talk about the food, and sip the wine our sommelier was presenting that night. Something about sitting around that table and the camaraderie we all shared during those meals reminded me of home. This recipe mixes in an influence of French flavors through the goat cheese in this deliciously creamy pasta sauce. **MAKES 2 TO 4 SERVINGS**

Handful of fresh basil leaves
Handful of fresh flat-leaf parsley, plus
   more for garnish
⅓ cup pine nuts
2 garlic cloves
½ teaspoon salt

⅓ cup olive oil
½ pound angel hair pasta
4 ounces soft goat cheese
⅓ cup heavy cream
Crushed red pepper

COMBINE the basil, parsley, pine nuts, garlic, and salt in a food processor on high speed and slowly pour in the oil. Puree until the pesto is smooth. Set aside.

BRING a large pot of water to a boil, add the pasta, and cook to your preferred doneness, stirring occasionally. Reserve some of the pasta water for the pesto sauce, then drain the pasta in a colander and set aside.

COMBINE the goat cheese and heavy cream in a medium saucepan over medium-low heat, stirring constantly as the cheese melts into the cream. When the cheese is melted, about 3 minutes, add the pesto and 2 or more tablespoons pasta water to loosen it up. Stir until smooth.

ADD the pasta to the saucepan and toss with the pesto. Top with crushed red pepper, garnish with parsley, and serve.

Linguine Vongole

JAKE: This is my favorite pasta dish. Anytime I see linguine and clams on a menu, I order it. So I finally decided to try and make my own version, using lots of garlic, hot Italian turkey sausage, white wine, and clams. The secret addition is gumbo filé, which adds an extra punch of flavor and is of course a nod to my family from Louisiana!

MAKES 4 TO 6 SERVINGS

---

1 recipe Homemade Linguine (page 42)
    or 1 pound store-bought
2 tablespoons salted butter
Extra-virgin olive oil
10 garlic cloves, minced
¼ cup finely sliced green onions (white
    parts only)
1 hot Italian turkey sausage, casing
    removed
1 tablespoon dried basil

½ tablespoon dried oregano
1 teaspoon crushed red pepper
3 pounds littleneck clams, cleaned
1 cup dry white wine
1 teaspoon gumbo filé
¼ teaspoon salt
2 tablespoons chopped fresh flat-
    leaf parsley, plus more for garnish
    (optional)
Grated Parmesan (optional)

BRING a large pot of water with a splash of oil to a boil, add the pasta, and cook to your preferred doneness, stirring occasionally. Drain in a colander and set aside.

MEANWHILE, in a large skillet over high heat, melt the butter in 2 tablespoons oil. Add the garlic and green onions and sauté until they are crisp and deep brown, about 4 minutes. Add the sausage, breaking it up into small pieces with a wooden spoon, along with the basil, oregano, and crushed red pepper, and cook for about 3 minutes, until the turkey has cooked through. Add the clams and immediately pour in the wine.

COVER the pan and cook until all the clams open up, about 10 minutes, shaking the pot occasionally to encourage the clams to open. When all the clams have opened (discard any that do not), stir in the gumbo filé and salt and cook, uncovered, until the liquid has reduced slightly, about 4 minutes.

TOSS in the pasta and cook for about 1 minute to season it with the clam sauce. Stir in the parsley and, if desired, sprinkle with Parmesan and garnish with more parsley.

Fried Lobster Pasta

JUSSIE: I don't feel the need to even explain this dish. It's pasta. It's lobster. It's fried. Live your best life, people. Live your life.

MAKES 4 TO 6 SERVINGS

PASTA AND VODKA SAUCE

½ recipe Homemade Linguine (page 42)
    or ½ pound store-bought
1 tablespoon salted butter
1 tablespoon olive oil
1 shallot, minced
4 garlic cloves, minced
½ teaspoon crushed red pepper
1 teaspoon dried basil
1½ teaspoons kosher salt
Two 14.5-ounce cans no-salt-added
    diced tomatoes

½ cup vodka
½ cup heavy cream

FRIED LOBSTER BITES

Two 6-ounce fresh or frozen raw lobster
    tails, thawed if frozen
Kosher salt
½ cup unbleached all-purpose flour
Vegetable oil, for frying
Handful of fresh basil, chopped
Grated Parmesan

BRING a large pot of water to a boil, add the pasta, and cook to your preferred doneness, stirring occasionally. Drain in a colander and set aside.

MEANWHILE, start on the vodka sauce. Melt the butter in the oil in a large high-sided saucepan or Dutch oven over medium-high heat. When hot, add the shallot, garlic, crushed red pepper, basil, and salt and sauté until the shallot and garlic are about to get crunchy and crisp, about 2 minutes. Add the tomatoes, vodka, and cream, bring to a simmer, and cook over low heat, uncovered, until the tomatoes have completely broken down to a thick sauce, about 20 minutes.

WHILE the sauce simmers, begin frying up the lobster bites. Remove the lobster meat from the shell (you can ask the fishmonger to do it for you). Slice the lobster tail down the back, giving you 2 long pieces of lobster meat. Dice the meat into small popcorn-size pieces. Transfer these lobster bites into a zip-top bag, add ¼ teaspoon salt and the flour, seal the bag, and toss the lobster to coat completely.

LINE a plate with paper towels and set aside. Heat 2 inches of oil in a large cast-iron skillet or heavy-bottomed frying pan over high heat until very hot. (Sprinkle a little flour in the oil and if it sizzles, the oil is ready.) Working in batches so as not to overcrowd the skillet, fry the lobster bites for 3 to 5 minutes, until golden brown and crisp. Place the lobster on the prepared plate to drain. Season immediately with salt.

ADD the pasta to the sauce and toss to let all that deliciousness season the noodles. Place the pasta in a large serving bowl and top with basil, Parmesan, and those tasty little fried lobster bites.

Family time is a big part of our lives!
We love creating new memories.

Cheesy Herb Manicotti Casserole

JURNEE: Growing up, we had our own way of doing everything—our own way of dressing, our own rules for games, and our own way of being "on time." We had our own language, our own inside jokes—we were our own little nation. Of course we didn't realize it then. We even had our own way of eating manicotti. I mean, doesn't everyone slice open their pasta tubes? Wait, what? Most people *stuff* their pasta tubes? So strange . . . well, here's to starting a manicotti revolution. Hope you enjoy this as much as we do. *Besos!*

MAKES 8 TO 10 SERVINGS

CASSEROLE

Two 8-ounce packages manicotti pasta
    shells
4 cups shredded sharp white Cheddar
    (about 1 pound)
2 cups shredded smoked Cheddar
    (about 8 ounces)
Nonstick cooking spray
¼ cup whole milk

PESTO

¼ cup chopped fresh oregano
⅓ cup chopped fresh basil

2 tablespoons pine nuts
¼ cup whole milk
1½ tablespoons finely grated Parmesan
¼ teaspoon sea salt

CRUNCHY TOPPING

1½ teaspoons dried basil
1½ teaspoons dried oregano
1 teaspoon crushed red pepper
½ cup finely grated Parmesan
½ cup panko bread crumbs
2 tablespoons unsalted butter, melted

PREHEAT the oven to 350°F.

BRING a large pot of water to a boil, add the manicotti, and cook to your preferred doneness, stirring occasionally. Drain in a colander and set aside.

MIX together the two types of shredded cheese in a large bowl.

TO make the pesto, pulse all the ingredients in a food processor until the mixture has a paste-like consistency.

MIX together the crunchy topping ingredients in a medium bowl.

SPRAY a 9 × 13-inch baking dish with the nonstick spray. Slice open all the manicotti tubes and make a flat pasta layer in the baking dish, then a layer of the cheese blend (you will use one fifth the pasta and one fifth the cheese in each layer). Follow with a second layer of pasta and cheese. Add a third layer of pasta, then a layer using all the pesto, then a layer of cheese. Next, add a fourth layer of pasta and cheese, then a fifth layer of pasta and cheese.

SPRINKLE the top with the crunchy goodness, then pour the milk carefully around the edges of the pan. Bake for 30 to 35 minutes, until the topping is browned and crisp.

Family-Style Lasagna

JURNEE: George Benson's *Breezin'* album playing on the record player and the smell of cheese, fresh herbs, lots of garlic, and Roma tomatoes baking in the oven. Nothing more comforting than a big casserole of Mommy's lasagna. We like to use turkey as an alternative to beef for this recipe, as beef can sometimes weigh it down. The secret to this dish is in the fresh Roma tomato sauce and the turkey sausage. A classic. Serve with fresh bread.

MAKES 8 TO 10 SERVINGS

---

2 tablespoons olive oil, plus more for greasing

18 garlic cloves, minced

¼ yellow onion, finely diced

2⅓ cups chopped cremini mushrooms

¼ cup chopped fresh basil, plus ⅓ cup for garnish

¼ cup dried basil

¼ teaspoon sea salt

5 hot Italian turkey sausages, casings removed

1½ pounds ground turkey

7 Roma tomatoes, cored and halved

⅓ cup tomato paste

1 pound lasagna noodles

2 pounds cottage cheese

4 cups shredded Monterey Jack cheese (about 1 pound)

4 cups shredded white Cheddar cheese (about 1 pound)

PREHEAT the oven to 375°F.

HEAT the oil in a large Dutch oven or saucepan over medium-high heat. Add the garlic, onion, mushrooms, fresh and dried basil, and salt and sauté until the vegetables are softened, 4 minutes. Add the sausage and ground turkey, breaking it up with a wooden spoon and stirring to combine. Cook the mixture until the meats are opaque and cooked through, about 12 minutes, stirring often.

PLACE the tomatoes in a blender and puree until completely smooth. Add the tomato puree and tomato paste to the Dutch oven and cook until thickened slightly, 5 minutes. Set aside to let cool slightly.

MEANWHILE bring a large pot of water to a boil, add the pasta, and cook to your preferred doneness, stirring occasionally. Drain in a colander.

ASSEMBLE the lasagna in a deep 9 × 13-inch casserole dish. Begin with a layer of noodles, using about 4 noodles to cover the bottom of the dish. Spread one quarter of the cottage cheese over the noodles, followed by one quarter of the sauce. Sprinkle 1 cup each of the Monterey Jack and white Cheddar cheeses. Repeat to make 3 more layers, for 4 total layers.

COVER and bake for 30 minutes. Uncover and bake 15 minutes more, or until the cheese is melted and bubbly. Let cool slightly to firm up, garnish with the basil, then slice and serve.

Green Pea Gnocchi with Parmesan White Wine Sauce

JAZZ: Gnocchi made its entrance into our family rather late; I did not try this little gem of a pasta until I was an adult. When I moved back to New York for college, I tasted it for the first time and found it to be really interesting. I started playing around with different versions of it, and this is by far the best I've had. It's made with both potatoes and green peas so it has an extra kick of flavor that is taken to another level by the wine and cheese sauce it's paired with. Yes, I said wine and cheese. I know, two of my favorite things ever!

MAKES 6 TO 8 SERVINGS

GREEN PEA GNOCCHI

1½ pounds Yukon Gold potatoes (about 3 medium to large potatoes)
1 pound frozen peas, thawed
1 large egg
1 teaspoon sea salt, plus more for salted water
½ teaspoon freshly ground black pepper
2 cups unbleached all-purpose flour, plus more for rolling out the dough

PARMESAN WHITE WINE SAUCE

4 tablespoons (½ stick) salted butter
6 garlic cloves, minced
1 cup dry white wine, such as Pinot Grigio or Chardonnay
2 teaspoons dried basil
¼ teaspoon crushed red pepper
1 cup heavy cream
1 cup grated Parmesan, plus more for garnish

TO make the gnocchi, place the potatoes in a large saucepan and cover completely with cold water. Bring to a boil, then reduce the heat and simmer for about 1 hour, until knife tender. Remove the potatoes from the boiling water (don't drain the water) and set aside to cool, about 20 minutes.

MEANWHILE, cook the peas in the hot water for 2 to 3 minutes, just so they heat through. Strain the peas, place them in a blender, and blend until completely smooth.

PEEL the cooled potatoes with your fingers or a knife and push them through a ricer into a large bowl. Fold in the pureed peas,

egg, salt, and pepper, then stir in the flour. The mixture will feel very tacky to the touch.

GENEROUSLY dust a clean work surface, your hands, and a rimmed baking sheet with flour. Form about one third of the gnocchi dough into a log and place the log on the floured work surface. Using your fingers, roll out the dough until it forms a snake about 1 inch in diameter. Cut the dough into ½-inch pieces and place them on the floured baking sheet. Repeat to make the rest of the gnocchi, dusting your hands and the work surface with more flour if things get too sticky. Set aside while you make the sauce.

TO make the Parmesan white wine sauce, melt the butter in a high-sided skillet over medium heat. Stir in the garlic and cook for 2 minutes, until fragrant and golden brown. Add the wine, basil, and crushed red pepper, bring to a boil, and cook for 3 to 4 minutes, until the wine is reduced by about a third. Whisk in the cream, bring to a simmer over medium-low heat, and cook about 5 minutes, until the mixture thickens slightly, stirring often. Stir in the Parmesan until it is completely melted and incorporated.

BRING a large pot of salted water to a boil. Working in small batches, gently drop the gnocchi into the boiling water, stirring once to make sure the gnocchi don't stick to each other. The gnocchi are cooked when they float to the top of the water. Use a slotted spoon to remove the gnocchi to a clean baking sheet and repeat to cook the remaining gnocchi.

TRANSFER the gnocchi to a serving dish and pour the sauce over the cooked gnocchi, tossing to coat completely. Garnish with more Parmesan and serve.

Baby Hunter is taking notes on how to cut this gnocchi. Go, Uncle Jocqui!

Remixed Alfredo Pasta Bake

JURNEE: However Jake came up with this dish, he deserves an award! We're obsessed with this pasta—it's so filling and delicious and full of cheesy goodness. It's a take on a favorite comfort food classic from childhood, with some added ingredients that send our souls into a state of bliss. It stands well alone or with a salad on the side.

MAKES 4 TO 6 SERVINGS

½ teaspoon kosher salt, plus more to taste

1 pound rigatoni

1 tablespoon olive oil

2 mild Italian turkey sausages, casings removed

5 chicken breast tenderloins, cut into ½-inch cubes

¾ cup sliced baby bella mushrooms (about 5 mushrooms)

4 tablespoons (½ stick) salted butter

4 garlic cloves, minced

¼ cup chopped fresh basil

¼ teaspoon ground white pepper

8 ounces cream cheese

2 cups whole milk

2 cups grated Parmesan (about ½ pound)

2 cups shredded white Cheddar (about ½ pound)

PREHEAT the oven to 350°F.

BRING a large pot of salted water to a boil, add the pasta, and cook to your preferred doneness, stirring occasionally. Drain in a colander and set aside.

MEANWHILE, heat the oil in a large deep saucepan or Dutch oven over medium-high heat. Add the sausage and chicken and season with the salt. Cook the meat until it begins to brown, 2 to 3 minutes, breaking up the sausage into small pieces with a wooden spoon. Add the mushrooms and cook, stirring often, until the meat is cooked through and the mushrooms are soft, about 10 minutes. Transfer the mixture to a medium bowl and set aside.

DRAIN all the grease from the pan, return the pan to low heat, and add the butter. When the butter is melted and slightly bubbling, add the garlic, half the basil, and the white pepper. Stir and let the garlic sweat for 1 minute, then add the cream cheese and whisk until smooth. Slowly whisk in the milk and bring the mixture to a simmer. Add 1½ cups of the Parmesan and 1½ cups of the Cheddar, constantly whisking to get that smooth, Alfredo sauce consistency. When the sauce is thick and creamy, return the sausage and chicken mixture to the pan and add the cooked pasta. Fold together to completely coat everything with sauce, then season with additional salt to taste, if needed.

TRANSFER the mixture to a 9 × 13-inch casserole dish and top with the remaining Parmesan, Cheddar, and basil. Bake for about 35 minutes, until the cheese is melted, bubbling, and beginning to brown on top. Set it out to cool for 10 minutes, then enjoy!

Spaghetti and Chicken Meatballs

JAKE: The twist on this classic favorite is in the meatballs. Chicken is a really nice substitute for beef because it's lighter and it works really well with the secret ingredient in the meatballs—caper juice. The meatballs themselves could even stand alone as an appetizer, but add the pasta and tomato sauce and you have an epic pasta feast!

MAKES 6 TO 8 SERVINGS

SAUCE

18 Roma tomatoes, halved lengthwise
¾ cup dry white wine, such as Pinot Grigio
6 tablespoons tomato paste
¼ cup chopped fresh basil
3 tablespoons chopped fresh oregano
1½ tablespoons dried oregano
3 green onions, thinly sliced
¾ teaspoon sea salt

MEATBALLS

1½ pounds ground chicken (about 92% lean and 8% fat, or buy ground chicken made from dark meat)
5 slices applewood-smoked bacon
5 garlic cloves, minced
¼ onion, minced
1 tablespoon chopped fresh oregano
1 tablespoon chopped fresh basil
½ teaspoon salt
1 teaspoon dried basil
1 teaspoon crushed red pepper
½ cup processed grated Parmesan, such as Kraft
½ cup panko bread crumbs
1 teaspoon apple cider vinegar
3 tablespoons caper juice
2 to 3 tablespoons olive oil

PASTA AND GARNISH

1 pound spaghetti
Fresh basil, torn
Grated Parmesan

PUREE the tomatoes in a food processor until no chunks are left, 1 to 2 minutes. You may need to work in two batches. Set aside.

TO make the meatballs, put the chicken in a large bowl. Set aside.

LINE a plate with paper towels and set aside. Arrange the bacon in a large cast-iron skillet or heavy-bottomed frying pan over high heat and cook until crispy, 3 to 4 minutes on each side. Remove the bacon to the lined plate to absorb the excess oil. Reserve the bacon grease in the skillet. Return the skillet to high heat, add the garlic and onion and sauté for 3 minutes, or until golden brown. Add the fresh herbs and sauté for 3 minutes. Season with the salt and place the mixture in the bowl with the chicken. Sprinkle with the dried basil and crushed red pepper. Chop the bacon and add it to the bowl, then add the Parmesan, panko, vinegar, and caper juice. Mix with clean hands until fully incorporated (but don't overmix). Roll the meat mixture into 1-inch balls, using about

1 heaping tablespoon of the meat mixture for each. This should make about 40 meatballs.

USING the same skillet, set the heat to medium and add the oil. Working in batches so as not to overcrowd the pan, cook the meatballs for about 4 minutes on each side, until browned. Use a small spoon to turn them over. When the meatballs are browned all over, transfer them to a plate and repeat to brown the rest of the meatballs.

DISCARD all but 1 tablespoon of the pan grease and return the pan to low heat. Add the reserved tomato puree, the wine, tomato paste, fresh and dried herbs, green onions, and salt and stir. Scrape the bottom of the pan with a wooden spoon to release all the browned bits. Reduce the heat to a simmer, nestle all the meatballs in the sauce, and cook, uncovered, for 12 to 15 minutes.

BRING 4 quarts water to a boil, add the pasta, and cook to your preferred doneness, stirring occasionally. Drain in a colander, then transfer the pasta to the meatballs and sauce. Garnish with basil and Parmesan and serve.

THE GREAT
Outdoors

JAZZ: Some of the best times we had as kids were the Fourth of July barbecues at our godfather's house in Jamaica, Queens. The days never seemed to end. We'd sit on the back stoop for hours and hours, daydreaming with our godsister and her cousins. We imagined what planets we would want to rule and what secrets they held while holding burning sparklers until the very last light went out.

There were always lots of people gathered, and Dad and Uncle Zach would man the grill. Mom would sit with them, usually with a baby attached to her or in her belly. They would wait for the coals to settle into a light gray, then put on the meats, such as smoked Louisiana sausage, juicy bacon cheeseburgers, sweet baby back ribs, marinated chicken wings, and more.

We played endless games of freeze tag; red light, green light; and tag football—until we were sent to the store for more charcoal. Following our oldest brother and godsister to the store meant we could use our pocket change to get treats. It also meant listening to the two of them—both *Star Trek* obsessives—debate wild ideas of science fiction and tell elaborate stories that the rest of us were still young enough to believe. Those days were the wonder of childhood.

Now that we are adults, summertime still means grilling and endless parties that flow well into the night; our annual midnight barbecue has become legend.

Summer days are special, and there's something really magical about cooking food on an open fire well into the night. It's a primitive human experience and feels like the natural way to cook and commune with our favorite people. Here's to grilling up something worth savoring and hanging outdoors on those warm summer days and nights!

Honey-Sriracha Chicken Skewers

JAKE: These chicken skewers are my take on buffalo wings. Instead of wings, I use thighs, and instead of buffalo sauce, I use sriracha topped with blue cheese crumbles to give it that extra salty, cheesy kick. These skewers are super quick and easy to throw on the grill. And because they're made with dark meat, they're extremely tender and flavorful. Pair with Cajun Fries (page 149). **MAKES 6 SERVINGS**

3 tablespoons rice vinegar
2 tablespoons sriracha
1 tablespoon honey
1 teaspoon Dijon mustard
4 boneless, skinless chicken thighs
½ teaspoon paprika
½ teaspoon granulated garlic
½ teaspoon granulated onion

½ teaspoon sea salt
1 tablespoon olive oil
¼ cup crumbled blue cheese
Handful of fresh flat-leaf parsley, chopped

SPECIAL EQUIPMENT: skewers (if wooden, soak for 20 minutes before grilling)

CLEAN and oil the grill grates (I like to use the end of a cut onion dipped in olive oil to oil my grates) and preheat the grill to high.

IN a liquid measuring cup or small bowl, whisk together the vinegar, sriracha, honey, and mustard until smooth. Set aside.

CUT the chicken thighs into small square pieces, 6 to 8 pieces per thigh. Put the chicken in a large bowl and season it with the paprika, granulated garlic, granulated onion, and salt. Add the oil and mix to coat the chicken. Divide the chicken among the skewers.

GRILL the skewers until thoroughly cooked and slightly charred, 5 to 7 minutes on each side, lightly brushing the sauce over the skewers as they cook.

PLATE the skewers and top with blue cheese and parsley.

BLUEBERRY LEMONADE

One 12-ounce bag frozen blueberries
2 cups fresh lemon juice (about 8 large lemons)

¼ cup plus 2 tablespoons agave

Combine the blueberries and lemon juice in a blender and blend until the blueberries are completely broken down. Transfer to a large pitcher and stir in the agave and 2 quarts water. Serve over ice! MAKES 2½ QUARTS

Fall-off-the-Bone Slow-Smoked Ribs

JAKE: When I was growing up, my mom would bake baby back ribs in the oven for hours and they would come out so tender that the bone would fall out, so I became accustomed to incredibly tender ribs. Oh, the art of slow-cooking ribs on the grill to get that perfect pork dry-rubbed crust on the outside and tender juicy meat on the inside! I love baby backs as if they were a part of my family.

MAKES 2 TO 4 SERVINGS

½ tablespoon granulated garlic
½ tablespoon minced dried onion
½ tablespoon crushed red pepper
2 teaspoons ground cumin

2 teaspoons paprika
1 teaspoon dried oregano
1 teaspoon kosher salt
1 rack baby back pork ribs (13 to 16 ribs)

TO make the dry rub, mix together all the seasonings in a small bowl. Lay the rack of ribs on a large baking sheet and coat the whole surface with the dry rub, patting it in to cover thoroughly.

TO slow-cook the ribs, you'll need indirect heat. Here's how I do it: using a four-burner

gas grill, I turn two of the burners to low heat, place the ribs on the off burners, away from the heat source, and close the lid. Slow-cook the ribs for about 2 hours, or until perfectly tender. Check on the meat every once in a while, but mostly just patience is required.

FRESH LIME MARGARITA

¼ cup silver tequila
½ cup fresh lime juice (from 6 to 8 limes)

½ cup ginger ale
1 tablespoon agave

Mix together the tequila, lime juice, ginger ale, and agave in a shaker. Pour over ice and serve! MAKES 1 DRINK

Grilled Sausage Pita Pocket

JAKE: Living in Southern California, I grill year-round. I love being outside, just a man and his grill. Well, most times a man, his grill, a drink, and a bunch of people—but all the same, it's great. I love grilling up some of my childhood favorites, like this sausage pita with grilled onions and peppers. My mom used to do it in a skillet on the stove, but I thought it was time to bring it outside. **MAKES 4 SERVINGS**

½ yellow onion, cut into ¼-inch slices
1 yellow bell pepper, cored, seeded, and
    cut into ¼-inch strips
3 tablespoons olive oil
4 hot Italian pork sausages, butterflied

2 large pita pockets, halved, pockets
    opened
2 tablespoons spicy brown mustard
2 tablespoons mayonnaise
1 Roma tomato, thinly sliced
¼ head iceberg lettuce, shredded

CLEAN and oil the grill grates (I like to use the end of a cut onion dipped in olive oil to oil my grates) and preheat the grill to high.

TOSS the onion and pepper with the oil in a small bowl and transfer them to a perforated grill pan. Set the vegetables and sausages on the grill at the same time, leaving the grill uncovered.

COOK the sausages until charred grill marks appear, about 6 minutes, then flip and cook for about 4 minutes more, or until charred and cooked through. Toss the vegetables occasionally to cook them evenly. In the last few minutes of cooking, set the pita pockets on the upper grill rack to warm them through. Remove the vegetables, sausages, and pita pockets from the grill.

WHISK together the mustard and mayonnaise in a small bowl. Slather the inside of each pocket with the mixture, then insert a sausage into each pocket. Divide the grilled onions and peppers as well as the tomato slices and shredded lettuce among the four pockets and serve immediately.

Finger-Licking BBQ Bacon Cheeseburger

JAZZ: BBQ and bacon and cheese and burger! This gives me life. Make this at a cookout and summon all the nostalgia for roadside fast-food spots. This all-American restaurant-style burger pairs perfectly with our Cajun Fries (page 149) or Dill Potato Salad (page 157)

MAKES 4 SERVINGS

BBQ SAUCE
1 cup ketchup
¼ cup plus 1 tablespoon apricot preserves
2 tablespoons distilled white vinegar
2 tablespoons spicy brown mustard
1 tablespoon Worcestershire sauce
3 tablespoons adobo sauce

BURGERS
1 pound ground beef
1 teaspoon kosher salt
1 tablespoon Worcestershire sauce
2 teaspoons granulated garlic
2 teaspoons granulated onion
1 teaspoon ground white pepper
4 slices extra-sharp white Cheddar
4 large sesame seed buns
8 slices thick-cut bacon, cooked until crisp
1 small red onion, thinly sliced

CLEAN and oil the grill grates (I like to use the end of a cut onion dipped in olive oil to oil my grates) and preheat the grill to high. Whisk together the BBQ sauce ingredients in a small saucepan. Bring the mixture to a boil, reduce the heat to a simmer, and cook until the flavors marry, about 5 minutes. Cover to keep warm.

PUT the ground beef in a large bowl and season with the salt, Worcestershire, granulated garlic, granulated onion, and white pepper. Gently fold together to incorporate, then form the meat into four ¼-inch-thick patties.

GRILL the patties until char marks appear, 2 to 3 minutes per side for medium-well done, or to your desired doneness. Top with the cheese slices in the last minute and let them melt. Quickly toast buns on the grill until browned and crusty, about 1 minute.

ASSEMBLE the burgers with a couple slices of bacon, onion slices, and a slather of the BBQ sauce.

1980S VINTAGE ROOT BEER FLOAT

1 scoop Honey-Vanilla Ice Cream
   (page 229)

One 8-ounce bottle or can good-quality
   root beer, such as A&W

Place the ice cream in a large glass. Pour the root beer over it and enjoy! MAKES 1 DRINK

Pesto-Slathered Chicken Thighs

JAKE: This dish came about one summer when our brother Jocqui and I got a group of friends together to go beach camping off the California coast. We had all the meat prepped and marinating in a cooler, including a simple marinade on a bunch of chicken thighs. I grilled the thighs, and of course everyone wanted barbecue sauce. Well, I hadn't made any, but I did have a huge container of homemade pesto for pasta in the cooler. So I drizzled a bit of pesto over the grilled chicken, and we were all bone- and finger-sucking after the meal. It was the creation of grilled pesto chicken! We love eating this with mashed potatoes or potato salad.

MAKES 4 TO 6 SERVINGS

CHICKEN

8 bone-in, skin-on chicken thighs
2 teaspoons salt
2 teaspoons ground white pepper
2 teaspoons granulated onion
2 teaspoons granulated garlic
2 teaspoons dried basil
4 tablespoons olive oil

PESTO

½ cup chopped fresh basil
½ cup chopped fresh flat-leaf parsley
½ cup processed grated Parmesan, such as Kraft
½ cup pine nuts
6 garlic cloves
2 green onions, roughly chopped
10 tablespoons olive oil
1 teaspoon salt
4 tablespoons fresh lemon juice

CLEAN and oil the grill grates (I like to use the end of a cut onion dipped in olive oil to oil my grates) and preheat the grill to high.

PLACE the chicken in a medium bowl and season with the salt, white pepper, granulated onion, granulated garlic, dried basil, and oil. Toss to coat the chicken completely in oil and spices.

PLACE the chicken skin side up on the grill and immediately turn off the flame under the chicken, leaving the other part of the grill on, to cook the chicken over indirect heat. Don't move or flip the chicken. Cook the thighs until juices run clear and the skin is browned and crispy, about 45 minutes.

MEANWHILE, make the pesto. Pulse the fresh herbs, Parmesan, pine nuts, garlic, green onion, oil, and salt in a food processor until fully broken down and loose. Mix in the lemon juice.

SPREAD the tops of each thigh with a good slathering of pesto. Serve the remaining pesto alongside for extra dipping. Enjoy!

RUM PUNCH

One 750 ml bottle dark rum, such as
    Appleton
4 cups (1 quart) passion fruit juice
4 cups (1 quart) pineapple juice

1 cup fresh lime juice (from 10 to
    12 limes)
½ cup simple syrup (see page 223,
    without the mint)
2 tablespoons rainbow peppercorns

Stir together the ingredients with 4 cups water in a large pitcher. Serve over ice.
MAKES ABOUT 3 QUARTS

Asian Skirt Steak Skewers

JURNEE: When I was five months pregnant, my husband and I went on a babymoon to Hawaii. The hotel we stayed in had an amazing Asian fusion restaurant with some of the finest cuisine I've ever had. I fell in love with the skirt steak entree and must admit I ate more than my (and my baby's) fair share. When we returned home, the mama-bear cravings kicked in and I set out on a mission to master a recipe for deliciously sweet and flavorful Asian skirt steak. Perfect for any barbecue, these skewers are finger-licking good!

2 TO 4 SERVINGS

8 garlic cloves, crushed
2 tablespoons toasted sesame oil
¼ cup liquid aminos
Juice of 2 limes (about ¼ cup)
2 tablespoons chili-garlic sauce
1 tablespoon minced peeled fresh ginger
1 pound skirt steak, cut into 2-inch slices against the grain

1 small red onion, thinly sliced, for serving
Pickled ginger, for serving
Pickled jalapeño chiles, for serving

SPECIAL EQUIPMENT: skewers (if wooden, soak for 20 minutes before grilling)

CLEAN and oil the grill grates (I like to use the end of a cut onion dipped in olive oil to oil my grates) and preheat the grill to high.

WHISK together the garlic, oil, liquid aminos, lime juice, chili sauce, and ginger in a small bowl. Set the steak flat in a baking dish or place it in a gallon-size zip-top bag and pour the mixture over the steak. Either cover the dish with plastic wrap or seal the bag. Let the steak marinate in the fridge for 30 to 45 minutes, then divide the steak slices among the skewers.

GRILL for 4 to 6 minutes on each side, or until cooked to your liking, basting the skewers with leftover marinade. Serve immediately with sliced onion, pickled ginger, and pickled jalapeños on the side.

Pork Tenderloin with Apricot Dipping Sauce

JAKE: Pork doesn't need much love to taste good, but this tenderloin has plenty of it. Tons of herbs, garlic, and onions stuffed into the loin make for flavor and seasonings in every slice. I pair this tenderloin with an apricot and jalapeño jam that my uncle Ern makes. MAKES 4 TO 6 SERVINGS

PORK AND MARINADE
6 garlic cloves, smashed
3 tablespoons minced onion
½ tablespoon whole grain mustard
1 tablespoon apple cider vinegar
1 tablespoon dried basil
1 tablespoon dried oregano
½ tablespoon paprika
1 teaspoon kosher salt

2 tablespoons olive oil
1 pork tenderloin (about 1½ pounds)

DIPPING SAUCE
⅓ cup apricot preserves
1½ tablespoons chopped pickled
  jalapeño chiles, plus 2 tablespoons
  juice from the jar

CLEAN and oil the grill grates (I like to use the end of a cut onion dipped in olive oil to oil my grates) and preheat the grill to high.

BLEND the marinade ingredients in a food processor until smooth. Place the tenderloin in a large bowl and coat it all over with the marinade. Use a knife to make small 1-inch pockets all over the tenderloin and take care that the rub gets into the pockets.

PLACE the tenderloin on the grill and immediately turn the flame off under the tenderloin, leaving the rest of the burners on. Let the tenderloin cook over indirect heat for 30 minutes; you're looking for an internal temperature of 155°F. Remove the pork from the grill and let it sit for about 10 minutes.

WHILE the pork is cooking, whisk together the dipping sauce ingredients in a small bowl.

CUT the tenderloin into ¼-inch slices and serve it with the dipping sauce.

Black Bean Quesadilla

JUSSIE: All praise Jazz Smollett, the bean queen, helming from Washington Heights! (That's good, right, Jazz?) This is one of the dishes that I ask for pretty much whenever I know Jazz is cooking. She usually makes the 'dilla stovetop or even enchilada-style, but one day I showed up and made a joke that I only eat grilled food. Jazz, also being the queen of sarcasm, threw the quesadilla on the grill, and I've never eaten it any other way since. So if y'all like this . . . blame me. **MAKES 6 SERVINGS**

PICO DE GALLO
4 Fresno chiles, diced
½ cup distilled white vinegar
1 tablespoon sugar
1 red onion, cut into small dice
4 vine-ripened tomatoes, cut into small dice
¼ cup chopped fresh cilantro
Juice of 2 limes (about ¼ cup)
1 teaspoon sea salt

QUESADILLAS
Two 8.5-ounce cans lima beans, drained
Two 15-ounce cans low-sodium black beans, with the liquid
2 teaspoons granulated garlic
2 teaspoons granulated onion
½ teaspoon salt
6 large (burrito-size) tortillas
3 cups shredded Fontina (about ¾ pound)

CLEAN and oil the grill grates (I like to use the end of a cut onion dipped in olive oil to oil my grates) and preheat the grill to high.

TO make the pico de gallo, combine the chiles, vinegar, and sugar in a small bowl. Let sit for 1 hour, then drain and finely dice the chiles (discard the vinegar-sugar). Combine the diced chiles with the rest of the ingredients in a medium bowl.

PUREE the lima beans and black beans in a blender or food processor until completely smooth. Add the granulated garlic, granulated onion, and salt and process a few more seconds to mix well.

SPREAD ⅔ cup of the bean mixture on a tortilla, then sprinkle one side of the tortilla with ½ cup of the cheese. Fold the tortilla over the cheese. Continue assembling the rest of the quesadillas.

PLACE the quesadillas on the grill and close the lid. Grill until there are char marks, 2 to 3 minutes, then flip. Continue cooking until the cheese is melted, about 2 more minutes. Slice into wedges and serve with the pico de gallo.

Carne Asada

JAZZ: What's a cookout without a charred steak? We were introduced to *carne asada* through Mexican culture here in Los Angeles and first started eating it at friends' birthday parties and restaurants. Later Jojo, our oldest brother, began shopping at the local Vallarta supermarket and would buy pounds and pounds of it already seasoned and ready for the grill. We then graduated to seasoning and making it ourselves at home for our epic summer barbecues. Here is our version of this loved Latin American classic!

MAKES 6 TO 8 SERVINGS

MARINADE
Juice of 1 orange (about ¼ cup)
Juice of 2 limes (about ¼ cup)
2 tablespoons olive oil
1 tablespoon granulated garlic
1 tablespoon granulated onion
1 tablespoon ground cumin
1 tablespoon chili powder
2 teaspoons kosher salt

1 chipotle in adobo, plus 1 tablespoon
    adobo sauce

STEAK AND ACCOMPANIMENTS
2 pounds flap steak (flap meat)
Flour tortillas, for serving
Fresh chopped cilantro, for serving
Pickled jalapeño chiles, for serving
Sliced red onion, for serving

WHISK together the marinade ingredients in a large bowl. Add the steak and toss to coat. Cover and refrigerate for at least 4 hours or up to overnight.

CLEAN and oil the grill grates (I like to use the end of a cut onion dipped in olive oil to oil my grates) and preheat the grill to high.

REMOVE the steak from the marinade, letting the excess liquid drain off, and grill for about 4 minutes, until charred. Flip and cook for 4 minutes more for medium-well done, or longer depending on desired doneness, then let rest for 5 minutes and slice thin. Serve with tortillas, cilantro, pickled jalapeños, and onion slices.

Grilled Lobster Rolls

JAZZ: Here in Los Angeles, we go mad for food trucks. We follow them on social media, we hire them for birthday parties, and we attend outdoor events just for the food trucks. My husband and I once made the mistake of giving our then two-year-old daughter a delicious lobster roll from the famed Lobsta Truck and she became hooked, asking for them all the time! But that truck is not always near us, and spending seventeen dollars a pop for a two-year-old to eat lobster was not going to help my retirement plan, so we began experimenting and I soon realized that for seventeen dollars, I could actually make several lobster rolls. So the next barbecue I hosted, I made Jake create one for me, and he killed it! These buttery lobster rolls are so delicious because they have a slight char flavor that perfectly complements this delicate seafood.

MAKES 4 SERVINGS

---

4 tablespoons (½ stick) salted butter
6 garlic cloves, minced
¼ teaspoon crushed red pepper
Pinch of sea salt
1 lemon

Four 3-ounce lobster tails, meat
removed from the shells, each cut
into 2 strips
4 hot dog buns
Handful of fresh flat-leaf parsley,
chopped

CLEAN and oil the grill grates (I like to use the end of a cut onion dipped in olive oil to oil my grates) and preheat the grill to high.

MELT the butter in a large cast-iron skillet on the grill, then add the garlic, crushed red pepper, and salt. Cook until the mixture reaches a saucy consistency, about 6 minutes.

MEANWHILE, squeeze juice from half the lemon over the lobster meat. Place the strips of lobster onto the grill and cook for 2 minutes on one side, then dip each strip into the butter sauce. Transfer the strips back to the grill and cook for 2 minutes

more, or until the meat is no longer translucent.

TRIM the long sides off the hot dog buns so they resemble split-top rolls or New England hot dog buns. Place the buns on the top rack to warm while the lobster cooks.

TO assemble the lobster rolls, spread a little of the cooked garlic from the butter sauce inside each bun, then place 2 lobster strips in each bun. Drizzle with plenty of butter sauce and garnish with the parsley. Serve with the remaining lemon half cut into wedges.

NEW ORLEANS
Roots

JAKE: There's no other city that reflects my family's history more strongly than the magical city of New Orleans. It's the resting place of my great-grandmother and my grandmother. Whenever I drive down the streets of Treme's Seventh Ward I can imagine my beautiful mother as a little girl sitting on her stoop or roller-skating through the neighborhood. Mom grew up with a single mother who worked day and night to provide for her four children but always somehow made sure dinner was served, and served well. Bean night was every Monday, and they would always have a weekend roast stuffed with tons of garlic and herbs. (I guess that's where I get my love for garlic.)

My uncle Michael, my mom's oldest brother, still lives in the city. The last time I visited him, the minute I got out of my car I smelled the red beans that he used to make when I was a kid. These red beans are famous in my family, and I knew the distinct smell of the ham hock (see the recipe on page 98). As I walked up to his front door, I said to myself, *It's Monday night. Of course he made beans—it's bean night!*

Keeping those traditions alive is what life's all about. New Orleans culture is strong and festive, with a huge importance placed on family, music, and food. The flavors of the culinary staples are as authentic and unapologetic as its people. You can find yourself eating a killer crab boil and a bowl of gumbo, then stumbling into a dope music set on Frenchmen Street and looking up at 4 A.M. still wanting more music and food. A constant sound track fills the city and makes you take life a little bit slower, or maybe I take it slow because I'm still drunk from the night before? That sounds about right. I love you, NOLA.

Seventh Ward Gumbo

JURNEE: We grew up with New Orleans in our blood, in our DNA, and it comes out in so many ways. I can remember well the aroma of Mommy's seafood gumbo filling the house, massive crab legs spilling out of her tall gumbo pot, sausage boiling, steam rising in her face as she stood over this tall pot, wooden spoon in hand, stirring in the "holy trinity" (onions, bell peppers, and celery). It was like watching a magician in her zone.

This recipe is a family table tradition on holidays such as Christmas and New Year's, and it's beloved by all of us. A bowl of Mommy's gumbo has always comforted us and brought us back to our happiest childhood roots. Mastering the family gumbo is a challenge in our household, which is never attempted lightly. This task has never even been handed to anyone younger than sixteen, and many of us never tried it until adulthood. Oddly enough, the key to a great pot of gumbo is in the consistency and strength of the roux. It can't be too thin or thick, and the color will dictate a lot. Once you master the roux, the rest of this one-pot meal comes together pretty quickly. **MAKES 10 TO 12 SERVINGS**

8 andouille sausage links, halved lengthwise and cut into ¼-inch slices

1 green bell pepper, cored, seeded, and minced

1 yellow bell pepper, cored, seeded, and minced

1 red bell pepper, cored, seeded, and minced

1 yellow onion, minced

16 garlic cloves, minced

3 celery stalks, minced

2 tablespoons vegetable oil

2 tablespoons salted butter

One 16-ounce bag frozen sliced okra, thawed

1 tablespoon dried basil

1½ tablespoons gumbo filé

4 quarts no-sodium chicken stock

1 tablespoon sea salt, plus more to taste

¼ teaspoon cayenne pepper, plus more to taste

4 bay leaves

¼ cup unbleached all-purpose flour

1½ pounds medium shrimp, peeled and deveined, tails removed

1 pound precooked snow crab claws

1 pound precooked snow crab legs

1 pound fresh or canned jumbo lump crabmeat, drained

Cooked white rice, for serving

FRY the sausages in a large stockpot over high heat for 10 minutes, or until crispy. Remove to a bowl. Drain the sausage grease and discard.

PUREE the bell peppers, onion, garlic, and celery in a food processor until smooth.

ADD the oil and butter to the stockpot and place it over high heat. Add the okra, and don't stir, letting it brown slightly. Stir after 6 minutes, then stir in the basil and gumbo filé, and cook for 2 minutes more. Add the vegetable puree and stir. This okra mixture turns into an "okra roux," giving it depth of flavor. Reduce the heat to medium, cover, and cook for 15 minutes. Add the stock (reserve 1 cup). Add the sausage. Season with the salt, cayenne, and bay leaves and bring to a boil, then reduce the heat and simmer for 1 hour.

WHISK together the flour and the reserved cup of stock in a small bowl. Pour the mixture into the pot, whisking constantly so the flour doesn't clump up. The roux should begin to thicken. Cover and cook for 30 minutes, stirring occasionally. Add the shrimp and crab claws, legs, and meat, cover, and cook for 30 minutes more, stirring occasionally. The roux should be dark brown and the consistency of a thick soup. Taste for seasoning and add more salt and/or cayenne if needed.

SERVE with white rice. The gumbo keeps well in the fridge for up to 2 days or in the freezer for up to 3 months.

Charbroiled Oysters

JURNEE: The first time I ate raw oysters was with my best friend, Talun, in San Francisco, and I've been obsessed with oysters ever since! I found myself searching restaurants far and wide to find the perfect oysters. When I'm eating oysters raw, I prefer them on the smaller, sweeter side, not too briny. My husband, on the other hand, isn't so keen on the idea of eating anything that's still alive (yes, raw oysters are still alive until you eat them, yikes!) and would often hesitate to even try them.

While shooting on location in Baton Rouge, our world was opened up to the brilliance that is charbroiled oysters. This is the perfect dish for any oyster lover as well as those who can't handle the idea of eating them raw. The mixture of textures with the crispy, crunchy crust and the soft center of the charbroiled oyster is just to die for. Interestingly enough, in this recipe I prefer using East Coast oysters, which tend to be larger and more briny, but use whichever you prefer.   MAKES 24 OYSTERS

½ pound (2 sticks) salted butter
16 garlic cloves
2 teaspoons dried oregano
½ teaspoon crushed red pepper

24 raw oysters, shucked in the shell
1 loaf French bread, halved lengthwise
½ cup chopped fresh flat-leaf parsley
½ cup grated Parmesan

CLEAN and oil the grill grates (I like to use the end of a cut onion dipped in olive oil to oil my grates) and preheat the grill to high.

BLEND the butter, garlic, oregano, and crushed red pepper in a food processor until completely smooth.

SCOOP 1 teaspoon flavored butter onto each oyster. Slather both halves of the bread with the remaining butter.

PLACE the oysters on the hottest part of the grill, directly on the grates. You want the grill to flame up around the oysters to melt the butter and charbroil the oysters. Place the bread on the upper grate of the grill, butter side up. Cook the oysters and toast the bread 5 to 6 minutes.

DURING the last minute of cooking, sprinkle the oysters with even amounts of parsley and Parmesan. When the cheese has melted slightly and the bread is nice and crusty, remove everything from the grill. Slice the bread and serve it with the oysters.

No one is a guest at our gatherings! They quickly become family. Then we can ask them to peel the garlic, or help set the table.

Oyster Po' Boys

JAZZ: New Orleans is known for its po' boys, and these are a staple in my family—our mom used to make them all the time. Here's my version that I'm passing on to you! I added slaw, but often they're topped just with ketchup, mayo, and a little lettuce. Try them both ways and see what you prefer. You'll have an excuse to eat two!

MAKES 6 SERVINGS

COLESLAW

⅓ cup mayonnaise
1 tablespoon distilled white vinegar
2 tablespoons fresh lemon juice
6 cups bagged carrot and cabbage mixture

OYSTERS

36 large oysters (about seven 6-ounce jars)
¾ cup yellow cornmeal
¾ cup unbleached all-purpose flour
1 teaspoon sea salt, plus more for sprinkling
1 teaspoon granulated garlic
1 teaspoon dried oregano
1 teaspoon dried basil
1 teaspoon paprika
½ teaspoon dried thyme
½ teaspoon granulated onion
½ teaspoon ground white pepper
½ teaspoon dried mustard
2 eggs, beaten
Vegetable oil, for frying

TO ASSEMBLE

6 French bread or bolillo sandwich rolls
Mayonnaise
Ketchup

WHISK together the mayonnaise, vinegar, and lemon juice in a large bowl. Add the carrot and cabbage slaw mix and toss to combine. Cover and refrigerate.

LINE a plate with paper towels, rinse the oysters, and let them drain on the lined plate.

MIX the cornmeal, flour, salt, granulated garlic, oregano, basil, paprika, thyme, granulated onion, white pepper, and dried mustard in a large bowl. Whisk the eggs in a medium bowl. Transfer the oysters to the egg mixture to coat, letting the excess drip off, then coat them one at a time in the dry mixture. Set aside.

LINE another plate with paper towels and set aside. Heat the oil in a large cast-iron skillet or heavy-bottomed frying pan over high heat until very hot. (Sprinkle a little of the dry spice mix in the oil and if it sizzles, the oil is ready.) Working in batches so as not to overcrowd the skillet, fry the oysters about 2 minutes on each side, until golden brown. Remove the oysters to the lined plate. While still hot, sprinkle them with salt.

PREHEAT the oven to 375°F.

SLICE open the rolls and warm them in the oven for 3 minutes. Spread both sides of the bread with mayonnaise and ketchup. Place 6 oysters on the bottom of each sandwich and top with coleslaw. Top the sandwiches and serve immediately!

CLASSIC HURRICANE

½ cup dark rum
1 cup white rum
½ cup grenadine

Juice of 4 limes (about ½ cup)
Juice of 4 oranges (about 1 cup)

Mix together all the ingredients with ½ cup water in a large pitcher. Pour over ice and serve! MAKES 1 QUART

Columbus Street Crawfish Boil

JUSSIE: When we were young, we didn't have much. I don't think we truly grasped just how broke we really were, but the love for one another and for food made us feel like billionaires. With that said, looking back, I can't believe that Mommy could pull out dishes like a crawfish boil. MAKES 6 TO 8 SERVINGS

1 pound purple, red, and white fingerling potatoes, scrubbed
½ cup Creole seasoning, more for serving
10 thyme sprigs
4 bay leaves
2 heads of garlic, outer skin only removed, halved crosswise
2 lemons, halved
One 3-ounce bag crawfish, shrimp, or crab boil seasoning, such as Zatarain's
1 yellow onion, quartered
1 pound andouille sausage, cut into 1-inch slices on the bias
2 ears sweet corn, shucked and cut into thirds
2 pounds live crawfish, rinsed (or, if necessary, use frozen and thaw first)
1 pound medium white Gulf shrimp, peel on, deveined
Kosher salt

COMBINE the potatoes, Creole seasoning, thyme, bay leaves, garlic, lemons, boil seasoning, and onion with 6 quarts cold water in a 14-quart or larger stockpot with a colander insert. Cover and bring to a boil, then reduce the heat and simmer for 10 minutes.

ADD the sausage and corn, cover, and simmer for 15 minutes. Add the crawfish, cover, and cook for 10 minutes. Add the shrimp and stir to combine, then cover and cook for 4 to 5 minutes, until the shrimp is opaque and cooked through. Carefully strain out the seafood, sausage, and vegetables by removing the colander insert from the pot and serve them on a large table covered with newspaper. Season with salt or additional Creole seasoning.

Cajun Shrimp Poppers

JURNEE: One thing the South can do better than any other place is fry food, and fried seafood is a favorite. Shooting in Baton Rouge, Louisiana, taught me the art of cooking this spicy popcorn shrimp. Treat yourself to this fast dish, served with a yummy horseradish dipping sauce.   MAKES 4 TO 6 SERVINGS

SHRIMP

2 pounds medium shrimp, peeled and
   deveined
1 teaspoon sea salt
2 teaspoons granulated onion
1 teaspoon granulated garlic
1 teaspoon paprika
¼ teaspoon cayenne pepper
3 eggs, lightly beaten

DRY SPICE MIX

1½ cups unbleached all-purpose flour
1 tablespoon granulated garlic
1 tablespoon plus 1 teaspoon granulated
   onion

2 teaspoons ground white pepper
½ teaspoon sea salt
½ teaspoon cayenne pepper
1 tablespoon plus 1 teaspoon paprika
1 tablespoon smoked paprika
1 tablespoon plus 1 teaspoon dried
   oregano

Vegetable oil, for frying

HORSERADISH DIPPING SAUCE

¼ cup ketchup
1 tablespoon mayonnaise
1½ teaspoons fresh lemon juice
½ teaspoon Louisiana hot sauce
1 tablespoon prepared horseradish

TOSS the shrimp with the salt, granulated onion, granulated garlic, paprika, and cayenne in a large bowl to evenly coat. Add the eggs and coat well.

WHISK together the flour, granulated garlic, granulated onion, white pepper, salt, cayenne, both paprikas, and oregano in a separate large bowl. Add the shrimp to the bowl and toss, making sure each piece of shrimp is coated well with the dry mixture.

LINE a plate with paper towels and set aside. Heat ⅛ inch oil in a large cast-iron skillet or heavy-bottomed frying pan over high heat until very hot. (Sprinkle a little of the dry spice mix in the oil and if it sizzles, the oil is ready). Working in batches so as not to overcrowd the skillet, fry the shrimp until they are golden brown and crispy on both sides, about 3 minutes total. Remove the shrimp to the lined plate to absorb the excess oil.

WHISK together the dipping sauce ingredients in a small bowl. Serve alongside your shrimp poppers!

Red Beans with Ham Hocks

JAZZ: As a kid, I spent many hot summer days in the kitchen with my mom, eating pickled pigs' feet from a jar and dousing them in hot sauce. It may sound strange to you, but in parts of the country it's very common to eat all parts of the pig, and a ham hock is simply the calf of the pig's leg, just above the foot. It's very flavorful and the perfect complement to red beans. I love this recipe because it cooks all day and I can laze around the deck, just checking it occasionally. I'm known among my friends and family as the bean queen, so naturally this recipe was passed on to me. It's the way my grandmother made her red beans and the way my mom, my aunt, my uncle, and I make them. They're delicious served over white rice.

MAKES 6 TO 8 SERVINGS, WITH LEFTOVERS

One and a half 16-ounce bags dried red
    kidney beans
18 garlic cloves, smashed
1 yellow onion, roughly chopped
2 celery stalks, roughly chopped
8 cups (2 quarts) chicken stock

2 ham hocks (about 2 pounds total)
¼ teaspoon cayenne pepper
Sea salt to taste
Handful of chopped fresh oregano
Cooked white rice, for serving

PLACE the beans in a large stockpot and add enough water to cover twice the height of the beans. Bring to a boil, then turn off the heat and let the beans sit, covered, for 1 hour. Drain the beans. Return the beans to the pot and again cover with water and bring to a boil. Turn off the heat, drain the beans, and return the beans to the pot. They will be softer but not fully cooked.

BLEND the garlic, onion, celery, and 2 cups of the stock in a food processor or blender until completely smooth, then transfer the mixture to the pot of beans. Add the remaining 6 cups stock and bring the liquid to a boil. Reduce the heat and simmer until the beans have softened further, about 1 hour. Add the ham hocks and cook until the beans are creamy and the hocks have broken down, 5 to 6 hours. Add the cayenne, taste, and adjust the seasoning with salt if needed (every ham hock and stock is different, so it's important to taste before adding salt). Garnish with the oregano and serve with white rice on the side.

Jake's Naked Fried Wings

JAKE: My mom tells a story of when she first met my dad in the Bay Area they would go to the movies, and instead of buying the overpriced refreshments at the theater, my mom would bring her homemade red beans and rice with fried chicken wings packed up in Tupperware. Well, she's certainly passed on the love of wings to me! To this day, if my mom is coming over to my house, I grab some wings and fry 'em up just how she likes them—wing tips on and fresh out of the fryer. We put the wings in a giant bowl and sit on the couch, Crystal hot sauce on deck, and we grub. This is our mother–son bonding time.

Just like my mom did for the movies, pair these with Red Beans with Ham Hocks (opposite).

MAKES 6 TO 8 APPETIZERS

½ cup Crystal hot sauce, plus more for serving

2 tablespoons granulated onion

2 tablespoons granulated garlic

2 teaspoons paprika

1 teaspoon cayenne pepper

2 teaspoons ground oregano

2 teaspoons ground thyme

2 teaspoons ground dry mustard

1 teaspoon fine sea salt

3 pounds tip-on chicken wings, split in two

Vegetable oil, for frying

COMBINE the hot sauce, granulated onion, granulated garlic, paprika, cayenne, ground oregano, ground thyme, ground dry mustard, and salt in a large bowl. Add the wings and toss to coat them completely.

HEAT 1 inch oil in a large cast-iron skillet or Dutch oven over high heat until very hot.

(Dip the end of a chicken wing into it and if it sizzles, the oil is ready.) Working in batches so as to not overcrowd the skillet, fry the wings until they turn a dark golden brown, about 9 minutes per side. Remove the wings to paper towels to drain.

SERVE with hot sauce!

Music, food, and celebration!

NOLA Smothered Chicken

JAKE: This dish embodies the soul of my mother's cooking. You can taste the love in the perfect dark brown gravy, in the time she took to really brown the chicken pieces to get that rich color and flavor. The chicken, garlic, onions, and celery are what really make the smothered chicken what it is. The herbs and spices take us back to our New Orleans roots, with the kick of heat from the cayenne. This chicken pairs well with Roasted Garlic Mashed Potatoes.

MAKES 6 SERVINGS

---

4 tablespoons (½ stick) salted butter
1 tablespoon extra-virgin olive oil
1 celery stalk, finely chopped
8 garlic cloves, minced
½ large onion, finely chopped
½ green bell pepper, cored, seeded, and finely chopped
¼ jalapeño chile, seeded and minced
8 bone-in, skinless chicken thighs
2½ teaspoons sea salt
1 tablespoon dried oregano

¼ teaspoon cayenne pepper
1 tablespoon gumbo filé
4 cups low-sodium chicken stock
⅓ cup unbleached all-purpose flour
10 baby bella mushrooms, finely chopped
Handful of fresh oregano, finely chopped
Roasted Garlic Mashed Potatoes (page 131) or cooked white rice, for serving

---

MELT the butter in the oil in a large heavy-bottomed pot or Dutch oven over medium heat. Add the celery, garlic, onion, bell pepper, and jalapeño and sauté until the mixture becomes the consistency of a roux, about 15 minutes. Add the chicken thighs and season them with 1½ teaspoons of the salt, the oregano, cayenne, and the gumbo filé. Let the chicken fully cook, making sure to create that nice golden-brown glisten, flipping halfway through, about 40 minutes total.

REMOVE the chicken to a large bowl and add 3 cups of the stock to the pan. All those delicious seasonings left in the pan will mix in with the stock, creating a tasty and time-friendly gravy. When the stock begins to simmer, add the remaining 1 cup of broth to a small bowl or liquid measuring cup. Whisk in the flour until smooth, then add the mixture to the pan, continuously stirring so it doesn't lump. Add the remaining 1 teaspoon salt and the mushrooms. Continue to cook until the gravy is smooth and thick, about 10 minutes, then return the cooked chicken to the pan, turn heat down to low, and simmer for 20 minutes more, until the chicken is married to the gravy.

GARNISH with the fresh oregano and serve with mashed potatoes or rice. It's a guaranteed hit for any occasion!

Spicy Stewed Okra with Sausage and Shrimp

JAKE: Okra has its origins in West Africa and made its way to the southern United States by way of slaves from the region. This dish has been passed down through generations and is still similar to the way it is prepared in West Africa. We've been making okra this way as far back as we can remember, and our mom learned from our grandmother and then passed it down to us.   MAKES 6 TO 8 SERVINGS

---

4 Louisiana hot sausage links, halved lengthwise and sliced into ½-inch pieces

1 pound medium shrimp, peeled and deveined, halved lengthwise (butterfly the shrimp but cut all the way through)

Two 12-ounce bags frozen sliced okra

10 garlic cloves, minced

½ yellow onion, finely diced

⅓ cup chopped fresh basil

⅓ cup chopped fresh flat-leaf parsley

⅓ cup chopped fresh oregano

Two 14.5-ounce cans no-salt-added diced tomatoes

2 tablespoons tomato paste

1 teaspoon paprika

½ teaspoon cayenne pepper

2 teaspoons kosher salt

Cooked white rice, for serving

PLACE a large cast-iron skillet or heavy-bottomed frying pan over high heat. Add the sausage and shrimp to the cold pan. Cook until the sausage is crispy and the shrimp is browned and opaque, about 5 minutes. Transfer the sausage and shrimp to a bowl, leaving the grease in the skillet, and set aside.

ADD the okra to the skillet, spread it out to cover the bottom, and then don't touch it, cooking until slightly charred, about 5 minutes. Stir and cook for another 3 minutes. Add the garlic, onion, and herbs and cook for 3 minutes. Add the tomatoes, tomato paste, paprika, cayenne, and salt. Stir and bring to a boil. Reduce the heat to low and simmer for 20 minutes, or until the tomatoes are broken down and stewed with the okra, stirring occasionally.

ADD the sausage and shrimp to the okra mixture and simmer for an additional 10 minutes.

SERVE hot with rice.

Crawfish Dip

JAKE: This easy crawfish dip will make you fall in love. One of my favorite memories growing up was going to the house of our longtime family friend Michael Criddle, where he'd have pounds and pounds of crawfish shipped in from New Orleans. He'd have his family and friends over to the house to grub on all the crawfish they could ever want. This crawfish dip was inspired by Michael's crawfish get-togethers. It's perfect served with tortilla chips. This one's for you, Mike! **MAKES ABOUT 2 CUPS**

---

1 tablespoon salted butter
6 garlic cloves, minced
1 pound fresh crawfish tail meat,
    chopped finely
2 tablespoons fresh lemon juice
3 green onions, finely sliced

½ cup mayonnaise
½ teaspoon sea salt
¼ teaspoon cayenne pepper
2 tablespoons minced celery
Tortilla chips, for serving

MELT the butter in a small saucepan over medium heat. Add the garlic and sauté until soft, about 1 minute. Remove from the heat.

PLACE the crawfish, lemon juice, green onions, mayonnaise, salt, cayenne, and celery in a large bowl. Add the butter and garlic and stir to combine. Transfer to serving bowls. Serve with tortilla chips.

SPECIALTY
Salads

JUSSIE: I love salads. My entire family loves salads. Growing up, there wasn't a time that we didn't have salad with a meal. Sometimes the salad *was* the meal. No matter where we moved, without fail there'd be a huge wooden salad bowl at the center of the table. It was not only the start of the food but also how we learned to cook. You can't burn a salad, and salads can't burn you. And when you show your creativity with the colors of the vegetables you use and by making your own dressing, you feel like your part matters to the meal.

The salad maker was the freshman and the meal makers were seniors. You can't roll up and start making grilled shrimp and veggie kabobs, Jake! Nah, bro. You don't just wake up and start making eggplant Parmesan, Jurnee! This is the starter, kid. This is the climb.

Since I'm older, I really take in all that Mommy says about the importance of staying healthy and eating as clean as possible. It's not some vanity thing—it's seriously important. To this day, my siblings and I get group texts from Mommy the length of a phone book telling us about the importance of "roughage," as she calls it. The text will usually start with something like "Hey, sweeties, Jussie has dark circles under his eyes and I feel the need to make sure that you kids are eating enough salads. . . ." Aside from the shade of calling us out, she'll go into a beautiful, long explanation of the need for green. The text usually ends with "I love you beyond the moon forever" followed by a bunch of emojis of hearts, fists up, and flags of Ghana and Great Britain (just go with it).

But she's made an impression, and we all believe salads are the wave of the future. They're healthy, keep you fit, and are inexpensive to make (a head of lettuce is ninety-nine cents), so if you don't mess with the green, let's see if we can change that. Ladies and gentlemen, I give you . . . salad!

FIVE MUST-HAVE SALAD DRESSINGS

JAKE: I always say a salad is only as great as its dressing. Knowing which salad needs a lighter versus a heartier dressing is key, so I offer salad pairings for my favorite five dressing recipes. These dressings are easy to make and perfect to keep in your fridge for your next great salad.

Balsamic Vinaigrette

Serve with Butter Lettuce Apple Crisp Salad (page 114).   MAKES ½ CUP

¼ cup olive oil	1½ teaspoons honey
¼ cup balsamic vinegar	Pinch of salt

WHISK together the ingredients in a small bowl or shake them in a jar. Store in the fridge for up to 30 days.

Blue Cheese Dressing

Serve over romaine lettuce or with Fatty Salad (page 121).   MAKES 1 CUP

½ cup buttermilk	1 tablespoon fresh lemon juice
½ cup blue cheese crumbles	½ teaspoon Worcestershire sauce

WHISK together the ingredients in a small bowl or shake them in a jar. Store in the fridge for up to 5 days.

Caesar Dressing

Serve over romaine lettuce or with Kale Caesar Salad (page 113).   MAKES 1 CUP

1 tablespoon minced anchovies	1 teaspoon Worcestershire sauce
⅓ cup olive oil	1 cup processed grated Parmesan, such
Juice of 1 lemon (about ¼ cup)	as Kraft

PUREE the ingredients in a food processor or blender until smooth. Store in the fridge for up to 5 days.

Chimichurri Sauce

Serve with a baguette or with Chimichurri Grilled Steak Salad (page 122).   MAKES 3 CUPS

4 cups chopped fresh flat-leaf parsley
10 tablespoons chopped fresh oregano
1⅓ cups chopped fresh cilantro
8 garlic cloves

4 green onions, roughly chopped
1 cup sherry vinegar
2 teaspoons sea salt
2 cups extra-virgin olive oil

BLEND the ingredients in a food processor or blender until smooth. Store in the fridge for up to 30 days.

Dijon-Lime Dressing

Serve with BlaVaMato Salad (page 117).   MAKES ¼ CUP

2½ tablespoons avocado oil
2 tablespoons fresh lime juice

1 teaspoon country Dijon mustard
¼ teaspoon salt

WHISK together the ingredients in a small bowl or shake them in a jar. Store in the fridge for up to 30 days.

Kale Caesar Salad

JAKE: Caesar salad is all about the dressing and the croutons. In this recipe I make giant garlic bread croutons from a French baguette, and the thick, cheesy dressing coats the kale in a way that will make you wanna slap yaself. I would pair this salad with Family-Style Lasagna (page 57). Go in!

MAKES 4 TO 6 SERVINGS

CROUTONS
One half 10-ounce French baguette, cut
    into 1-inch slices, then quartered
3 tablespoons salted butter
4 garlic cloves, minced

2 tablespoons processed grated
    Parmesan, such as Kraft

SALAD
5 ounces baby kale (about 3 cups)
Caesar Dressing (page 111)

PREHEAT the oven to 350°F.

PLACE the bread cubes in a large salad bowl. Melt the butter in a small skillet over medium heat, add the garlic, and cook until softened, about 1 minute. Pour the butter and garlic over the bread, add the Parmesan, and toss to combine. Spread the bread on a rimmed baking sheet and bake until golden brown, 10 to 12 minutes. Set aside.

PLACE the kale in the same salad bowl. Drizzle a small amount of the dressing over the kale and toss gently to lightly coat, using more dressing as needed. Top with croutons and serve.

Butter Lettuce Apple Crisp Salad

JAZZ: I first had this salad at Jake's house for a family get-together. I love Gorgonzola cheese, and it pairs beautifully with the Granny Smith apples. This salad is so refreshing! It goes well with pretty much any meal or as a light meal itself.

MAKES 4 SERVINGS

Head of butter lettuce, leaves separated and sliced in half

1 Granny Smith apple, peeled and shaved

¼ cup dried cranberries

¼ cup toasted chopped walnuts

½ cup Gorgonzola cheese crumbles

Balsamic Vinaigrette (page 111)

Freshly cracked black pepper

COMBINE the lettuce, apple shavings, cranberries, walnuts, and cheese in a large bowl. Drizzle a small amount of the dressing over the salad and toss gently to lightly coat, using more dressing as needed. Season with pepper and serve!

BlaVaMato Salad

JAKE: *BlaVaMato* stands for black bean, avocado, and tomatoes tossed together to make a killer mosh pit of a hearty salsa-inspired salad. It's fresh, easy to make, and pairs well with Fajita Chorizo Mexican Pizzas (page 180).

MAKES 4 TO 6 SERVINGS

1 pint assorted cherry tomatoes, halved
One 15-ounce can low-sodium black
   beans, drained and rinsed

1 Hass avocado, pitted, peeled, and diced
1 tablespoon chopped red onion
Handful of fresh cilantro, chopped
Dijon-Lime Dressing (page 112)

COMBINE the tomatoes, black beans, avocado, onion, and cilantro in a large bowl. Drizzle a small amount of the dressing over the salad and toss gently to coat. Add more dressing as needed. Serve cold.

Pickled Beet Salad with Burrata and Beet Green Pesto

JURNEE: Pickled beets were a family favorite growing up. Open our fridge and you'd usually find a large glass dish showcasing the beautiful bright beets and onions Mommy was pickling. This colorful beet salad with chunks of burrata cheese and this special beet green pesto complements a perfect summertime spread.

MAKES 4 SERVINGS

---

4 medium red beets, with greens
1 cup distilled white vinegar
1 tablespoon sugar
1½ cups fresh basil
3 tablespoons fresh lemon juice

¾ teaspoon pink Himalayan salt
¾ cup olive oil
4 heads red or white Belgian endive,
 leaves separated
Two 4-ounce burrata cheese balls,
 quartered

PREHEAT the oven to 375°F.

SEPARATE the beets from their tops, reserving the greens. Scrub the beets clean in running water, then peel and halve them lengthwise. Place the beets in a baking dish, add about ½ cup water, cover with a lid or foil, and steam in the oven until knife tender, about 40 minutes. Transfer the beets to a medium bowl. When cool enough to handle, cut the beets into 1-inch slices.

WHISK together the vinegar and sugar in a large bowl. Add the beets and toss gently. Cover with plastic wrap and refrigerate for at least 1 hour (feel free to make these up to 4 days ahead and keep them in the fridge). Drain the beets from the pickling liquid.

TO make the beet green pesto, puree 1 cup of the reserved beet greens, the basil, lemon juice, salt, and oil in a food processor until the mixture is broken down and almost smooth. If there is any extra, you can store it in the fridge for 2 to 3 days and use it as a spread for French bread.

ARRANGE the endive on a platter or individual plates and top with the beets, burrata, and a few dollops of the pesto.

Patty Salad

JAKE: You may think of salads as having a purpose—and that purpose is to get in your nutrients and vegetables for the day. But I think salads deserve to have a little fun, too, so we ditched the lean meat and vegetables for this one. We threw a fried chicken breast on top of a bed of crispy lettuce and topped it with bacon and topped that with a rich, creamy blue cheese dressing. It's to die for . . . but don't worry, you won't die. It's not that unhealthy.

MAKES 4 TO 6 SERVINGS

---

5 slices thick-cut bacon
1½ teaspoons sea salt
1½ teaspoons granulated onion
1½ teaspoons granulated garlic
1 teaspoon smoked paprika
¼ teaspoon ground white pepper
¼ teaspoon cayenne pepper
2 tablespoons fresh lemon juice
¾ cup buttermilk
1½ pounds boneless, skinless chicken
    breasts, cut into 1-inch cubes

½ cup white rice flour
Vegetable oil, for frying
Head of romaine lettuce, chopped
2 cups finely shredded purple cabbage
2 Persian cucumbers, cut into small dice
1 cup halved cherry tomatoes
1 Hass avocado, pitted, peeled, and cut
    into 1-inch cubes
⅓ cup finely chopped red onion
Blue Cheese Dressing (page 111)

LINE a plate with paper towels and set aside. Arrange the bacon in a large cast-iron skillet or heavy-bottomed frying pan over high heat and cook until crispy, 3 to 4 minutes on each side. Remove the bacon to the lined plate to absorb the excess oil. Reserve the bacon grease in the skillet. When the bacon is cool enough to handle, chop it roughly, then set aside.

COMBINE the salt, granulated onion, granulated garlic, paprika, white pepper, cayenne, lemon juice, and buttermilk in a large bowl. Toss the chicken in the mixture and let the pieces drain slightly on a paper towel. Dredge the chicken in the flour, tossing lightly to coat.

LINE a plate with paper towels and set aside. Add oil to the bacon grease, filling the skillet a quarter of the way up the side and place over high heat. Dip a piece of chicken in the oil and if it sizzles, the oil is ready. Working in batches so as not to overcrowd the skillet, fry the chicken until golden brown all over, 4 to 5 minutes, turning as needed. Remove to the lined plate to absorb the excess oil.

TO assemble the salad, toss the lettuce and cabbage in a large serving bowl. Add the cucumbers, cherry tomatoes, avocado, onion, bacon, and fried chicken. Drizzle the dressing over the salad and serve.

Chimichurri Grilled Steak Salad

JAZZ: Our mom always wanted to take the scenic route, especially when we drove to Oakland from Los Angeles. She didn't care that it took longer, because the beauty of the drive along the Pacific Ocean was well worth it. We'd always detour to Gilroy, California, known as the garlic capital of the world. We knew we were getting close to Gilroy when we'd start to see the huge open truckloads of garlic on the road in front of us. The smell of garlic growing in the fields was a feast for the senses. At the local shops we bought foods such as garlic-stuffed olives, garlic-infused olive oils, and roasted garlic salad dressings. Our love of garlic was definitely solidified on these trips.

I can think of no better way to use this brilliant aromatic than my current obsession, chimichurri sauce. This steak salad is way too good to resist. Hope you enjoy! Love and hugs.   MAKES 4 TO 6 SERVINGS

---

2 New York strip steaks (about 1½ pounds)
1 teaspoon kosher salt
1½ cups Chimichurri Sauce (page 112)
1 red bell pepper, cored, seeded, and sliced
1 yellow bell pepper, cored, seeded, and sliced

1 red onion, cut into ½-inch strips
Bunch of green onions
1 tablespoon olive oil
8 ounces baby arugula (about 8 cups)
¼ cup crumbled cotija cheese

SEASON the steaks with salt. Transfer to a zip-top bag or large baking dish and coat well with ¾ cup of the chimichurri sauce. Seal the bag or cover the dish and refrigerate for 45 minutes to 1 hour to marinate.

CLEAN and oil the grill grates (I like to use the end of a cut onion dipped in olive oil to oil my grates) and preheat the grill to high.

PUT the bell peppers and onion in a perforated grill pan, drizzle with the oil, and toss.

WHEN the grill is nice and hot, set the steaks and pan of veggies on the grill, leaving the lid open. Cook the steaks until charred and grill marks appear, about 6 minutes per side for medium-rare. (If you want yours more well done, add a couple of minutes per side.) While the steaks cook, turn the veggies to be sure all sides are hitting the heat and take care not to let the green onions burn. Remove the vegetables when you get a desired char on them. Pull the steak. Let the steak rest for 5 minutes, then cut it into ½-inch slices.

TO assemble the salad, pour another ½ cup chimichurri sauce into a large salad bowl, add the arugula, and toss gently to lightly coat. Evenly distribute the arugula among your serving dishes, then divide the steak and veggies over the arugula. Finish with a sprinkling of cotija cheese and a final drizzle of dressing over the steak.

THE BEST
Side Dishes

JAZZ: Here's to throwing caution to the wind with your side dishes. Feel free to explore cultural boundaries and color outside the lines when pairing sides with mains. Sides are not an afterthought but an opportunity to add unexpected surprises to the meal. Sides are also a great opportunity to contribute to a potluck dinner and impress everyone with what you bring to the party.

Smoked Cheddar and Creole Mac-n-Cheese

JURNEE: I like to use a combination of cheeses in my mac and cheese. I've experimented with several different types, and this version is hands down my favorite. I'm in love with the flavor of the smoked Cheddar, paired with the tinge of spice in the pepper Jack. Neither overpowers the other. I also prefer to use pasta shells, as they hold the cheese nicely. The key to this recipe is the béchamel sauce, which gives you a nice creamy, cheesy mac.

MAKES 6 TO 8 SERVINGS

---

1 pound medium pasta shells

2 tablespoons olive oil

2 cups panko bread crumbs

5 tablespoons unsalted butter

5 tablespoons unbleached all-purpose flour

2 cups whole milk

2 tablespoons Creole spice blend, such as Tony Chachere's Creole Seasoning

2 tablespoons dried dill

1 large egg, beaten

2 cups shredded smoked Cheddar (about 8 ounces)

2 cups shredded Monterey Jack (about 8 ounces)

2 cups shredded pepper Jack (about 8 ounces)

BRING a large pot of water to a boil, add the pasta, and cook to your preferred doneness, stirring occasionally. Drain in a colander and set aside.

MEANWHILE, heat the oil in a large cast-iron or heavy-bottomed skillet over medium-high heat. Add the panko and stir constantly with a wooden spoon, toasting until golden brown, about 4 minutes. Set aside to cool.

MELT the butter over medium heat in a large Dutch oven or heavy-bottomed saucepan. Add the flour and whisk vigorously to combine, taking care not to burn the mixture, 1 to 2 minutes. Gradually pour in the milk, whisking constantly to avoid lumps. Bring the béchamel to a simmer and cook, whisking, until thick enough to coat the back of a spoon, 4 to 6 minutes. Mix in the Creole spice blend and dill.

CRACK the egg into a medium bowl. Drizzle ⅓ cup of the béchamel sauce into the egg to temper it, whisking all the while. Return the egg-béchamel mixture to the pot and whisk to combine. Gradually add the Cheddar and Jack cheeses, whisking to maintain a smooth texture and avoid clumping. Stir in the cooked pasta.

SPOON the warm mac and cheese into a serving bowl. Top with the panko and serve.

Jalapeño-Bacon-Cheddar Corn Bread

JURNEE: Texas might be known for its barbecue, but I'll forever think of Texas when I make this corn bread. I was shooting a TV show with too many days off, which meant I spent much of my time wandering around the city. If Austin is known for nothing else, it's known for its live music scene and its food. It was there that I discovered the joy of eating jalapeño corn bread—moist, with a touch of sweet and spice. Such an original take on traditional corn bread.

MAKES 10 TO 12 SERVINGS

---

6 slices center-cut applewood-smoked bacon
2 jalapeño chiles, seeded and finely diced
2 cups cornmeal
2 cups unbleached all-purpose flour
1½ cups light brown sugar
2 teaspoons baking powder

1 teaspoon kosher salt
2 cups buttermilk
¾ cup vegetable oil
2 large eggs, lightly beaten
½ pound white Cheddar, shredded (about 2 cups)
2 tablespoons unsalted butter, melted

PLACE a rack in the center of the oven and preheat the oven to 350°F.

LINE a plate with paper towels and set aside. Arrange the bacon in a large cast-iron skillet or heavy-bottomed frying pan over medium-high heat and cook until crispy, 3 to 4 minutes on each side. Remove the bacon to one end of the lined plate to absorb excess oil (save room for the jalapeños!). Reserve the bacon grease in the skillet. Add the jalapeños to the bacon drippings in the skillet and sauté until softened and slightly browned, about 4 minutes. Using a slotted spoon, transfer the jalapeños to the plate next to the bacon. Roughly chop the bacon and return it to the plate.

CAREFULLY remove 2 tablespoons of the bacon drippings from the pan, leaving the rest. Keep the pan at the ready for baking the corn bread.

COMBINE the cornmeal, flour, brown sugar, baking powder, and salt in a large bowl.

WHISK together the buttermilk, oil, and eggs in a medium bowl. Add the buttermilk mixture to the cornmeal mixture and use a rubber spatula to fold the dry ingredients into the wet until incorporated (do not overmix). Mix in the cheese, bacon, and jalapeño.

USING a pastry brush, spread the bacon drippings up the sides and around the

bottom of the skillet. Heat the skillet over medium-low heat, until the fat just starts to sizzle. Pour in the corn bread batter and keep the pan on the heat for a minute to set the bottom crust.

BAKE until golden brown and a wooden skewer inserted into the middle of the corn bread comes out clean, 45 to 50 minutes. Baste the top crust with the butter. Cool for 20 minutes before serving.

Pancetta–Pomegranate Brussels Sprouts

JURNEE: I reject the notion that Brussels sprouts are boring. Prepare them right and they'll be the surprise star of the meal. This is my favorite way to prepare Brussels sprouts, with the pancetta and pomegranate adding salty and sweet elements. Prove any Brussels sprouts hater dead wrong with this easy dish that bursts with flavor.

MAKES 8 TO 10 SERVINGS

1 tablespoon salted butter
1 tablespoon extra-virgin olive oil
1 cup cubed pancetta (about 8 ounces)
¼ cup finely chopped red onion

½ cup fresh pomegranate seeds
¼ cup rice wine vinegar
4 pounds small fresh Brussels sprouts, trimmed and halved
½ teaspoon sea salt

MELT the butter in the oil in a large high-sided, heavy-bottomed pan over medium heat. Add the pancetta, onion, pomegranate seeds, and vinegar and cook until the pancetta has crisped and the pomegranate seeds are softened, about 6 minutes, stirring frequently. Add the Brussels sprouts and toss to incorporate. Season with the salt. Cook the sprouts, stirring occasionally, until they are softened and browned, about 12 minutes. (I like mine with a little bite! Leave them cooking with the pan covered for a bit if you prefer softer sprouts.)

Roasted Garlic Mashed Potatoes

JURNEE: I love freshly roasted garlic. The aroma it brings to any dish is unrivaled. It's surprisingly easy to make. In the past, I've used it as a spread on bread, in pasta, and now in these mashed potatoes. It adds a subtle flavor, a nice variation to this classic dish. **MAKES 4 TO 6 SERVINGS**

---

6 garlic cloves

Extra-virgin olive oil

2 pounds russet potatoes, peeled and cut into 2-inch dice (about 6 cups)

1 cup whole milk

8 tablespoons (1 stick) salted butter

1 teaspoon sea salt

½ teaspoon ground white pepper

1 green onion, thinly sliced

PREHEAT the oven to 350°F.

SPREAD the peeled garlic cloves on a rimmed baking sheet and drizzle with a little oil. Roast for 15 to 20 minutes, until the garlic is soft.

PLACE the potatoes in a medium saucepan and cover them with water. Bring to a boil, then reduce the heat and simmer for about 30 minutes, until knife tender.

DRAIN the potatoes and transfer them to a blender or food processor. Puree the potatoes with the milk and roasted garlic until just smooth, being careful not to overwork the mixture. Transfer the mashed potatoes back to the pot and add the butter. Stir until the butter has melted completely. Add salt and white pepper and mix the potatoes until smooth. Top with sliced green onion.

Let the festivities begin!

Potato Latkes

JAZZ: I learned to make these latkes from my grandmother when she last came to visit from New Mexico. She is eighty-six years old, travels alone, and is as spunky as can be. She stood in the kitchen with me to be sure I was doing it right and gently injected specific instructions when I veered too far off course. The two generations between us caused confusion when she kept asking if I had a box grater. Turns out she expected me to hand-grate almost five pounds of potatoes! That is what a food processor is for. We had a great time, though, and I'm grateful for this recipe—they turned out so good, and now I know how to make latkes! Thanks, Grandmolly!

MAKES ABOUT 28 LATKES

---

4 large russet potatoes, scrubbed and grated

2 large yellow onions, grated

2½ teaspoons kosher salt

2 teaspoons freshly cracked black pepper

1 egg plus 1 egg white, beaten

3 tablespoons unbleached all-purpose flour

Vegetable oil, for frying

Sour cream, for serving

Applesauce, for serving

COMBINE the grated potatoes and onions in a colander and press to remove as much water as possible. Transfer them to a large bowl, using both hands to squeeze out even more water as you go. Add the salt, pepper, egg and egg white, and flour and fold to combine.

HEAT ¼ inch oil in a large cast-iron skillet or heavy-bottomed frying pan over high heat until very hot. (Drop a piece of potato in the oil and if it sizzles, the oil is ready.)

LINE a plate with paper towels and set aside. Using two soup spoons, scoop out about 2 tablespoons of the potato mixture and form it into a patty. Place it in the oil and flatten the center so the patty is evenly thick. Working in batches so as not to overcrowd the skillet, make more latkes and fry until deep golden brown, about 3 minutes per side. (As you get to the bottom of the bowl, liquid will have leached from the potato mixture—squeeze it out!) Remove the fried latkes to the lined plate to absorb the excess oil.

SERVE immediately with sour cream and applesauce on the side!

Spicy West African Black-Eyed Peas

JUSSIE: I've always known about the tradition of eating black-eyed peas on New Year's Day. It represents prosperity and new beginnings. But did y'all know that the BEP, originally called a cow pea, originated in Africa? Year after year it can get tiring to eat black-eyed peas the same way, so it's fun to find new ways of remixing them. This version is sure to be a crowd favorite.   MAKES 8 TO 10 SERVINGS

1 pound dried black-eyed peas, sorted
    and rinsed
½ yellow onion, roughly chopped
8 garlic cloves, smashed
5 Roma tomatoes, cut into eighths
2 habanero chiles, halved and seeded
3 tablespoons olive oil

Sea salt
¼ cup tomato paste
1 teaspoon granulated garlic
1½ teaspoons smoked paprika
2 bay leaves
3 chicken bouillon cubes
½ teaspoon cayenne pepper

PLACE the beans in a large stockpot and cover with water. Bring to a boil and cook for 2 minutes. Remove from the heat, cover, and set aside to soak for 1 hour.

MEANWHILE, preheat the broiler to high. Place the onion, garlic, tomatoes, and habaneros on a rimmed baking sheet and toss with the oil and ½ teaspoon salt. Broil until the vegetables are charred and slightly softened, 5 to 6 minutes, rotating often. Transfer the broiled mixture to a blender and puree until smooth.

AFTER an hour of soaking, drain the beans, return them to the pot, and cover with 6 cups water. Bring to a boil, then reduce the heat and simmer, covered, until the beans are tender, about 30 minutes. Add the vegetable puree to the pot along with the tomato paste, granulated garlic, 1 teaspoon of the paprika, 2 teaspoons salt, the bay leaves, and the bouillon and stir. Bring to a boil, then reduce the heat again and simmer, covered, for 2 hours, stirring occasionally until the liquid is reduced to the consistency of a stew and the beans are soft and tender. Remove from the heat and stir in the remaining ½ teaspoon paprika and the cayenne. Adjust the seasonings to taste and serve.

Family Collard Greens

JURNEE: I worked throughout my pregnancy, and shooting on location in Savannah, Georgia, proved challenging for many reasons. Most of my pregnancy cravings were for foods I had grown up eating in my childhood. I found myself in the kitchen one day, trying to figure out how to make collard greens, a dish I had eaten on many occasions but had never made before.

One thing to note is it's very important to wash the greens thoroughly during prep. These greens require tender loving care, yet the process is really simple when mastered. This is my super simple but delicious recipe.

MAKES 4 TO 6 SERVINGS

---

4 bunches of collard greens, washed and stems removed, sliced into 1-inch strips

2 whole smoked turkey drumsticks (about 1¼ pounds total)

1 tablespoon apple cider vinegar

1 shallot, diced

½ teaspoon sea salt

⅛ teaspoon cayenne pepper

PLACE the greens in a large stockpot and add 2 cups water. Bring to a boil, then reduce the heat and simmer, uncovered, for 20 minutes, stirring often, until the collards have wilted. Add the turkey legs, vinegar, shallot, salt, and cayenne and cover, cooking until the meat is falling off bone and the collards are tender, 3½ hours. Remove the turkey legs, shred the meat, and discard the bones. Return the meat to the pot and serve immediately.

Spicy Smoked Gouda Twice-Baked Potatoes

JURNEE: I love to host parties, and one thing you can be guaranteed of at my house is an extravagant cheese plate to snack on. I've gained the reputation of being able to throw down on my cheese plates . . . and they are kinda amazing, if I do say so myself. A necessity for any party.

A staple for my cheese plate is my spicy Gouda dip. It's a favorite among my family and friends and usually the first to go. So I decided to change it up and combine two of my favorite things—spicy Gouda and potatoes! These are super easy to make; your fam and friends will be impressed and unable to stop praising your genius potato skills.

MAKES 4 SERVINGS

---

4 russet potatoes, scrubbed

4 cups grated smoked Gouda (about 1 pound)

1 cup mayonnaise

¼ cup sour cream

½ cup chopped pickled jalapeño chiles

1 green onion, thinly sliced, plus more for garnish

½ teaspoon smoked paprika

PREHEAT the oven to 400°F.

PLACE the potatoes directly on the middle oven rack and bake until knife tender, fluffy on the inside, and crispy on the outside, 1½ hours. Remove from the oven and set aside to cool. Turn the broiler to high.

MEANWHILE, stir together 2 cups of the Gouda, the mayonnaise, sour cream, pickled jalapeños, green onion, and paprika in a large bowl.

WHEN the potatoes are cool enough to handle, slice them open lengthwise, scoop out the fluffy insides, and carefully transfer them to the Gouda mixture. Fold gently to combine.

LAY the empty potato skins on a rimmed baking sheet and evenly distribute the potato filling among the skins, so they are almost overflowing with filling. Top each potato with a generous sprinkling of the remaining shredded Gouda.

BROIL the potatoes until the cheese is melty and gooey, about 4 minutes. Keep an eye on them so the cheese doesn't burn. Garnish with more green onions if desired. Serve immediately.

Asparagus and Mozzarella Pasta Salad

JAKE: Jurnee called me one day to say she was throwing Jazz's wedding shower and she wanted the brothers to make the food for it, so we took the job of catering for about twenty women with a one-day notice. I just went wild with all the fresh ingredients I put in this pasta salad. It was a hit! But then my brothers and I were asked to leave the party after the food was ready . . . women only. Two things I learned that day: pasta salad is just a mosh pit of great ingredients, and my sisters just used us to cook.

MAKES 6 TO 8 SERVINGS

---

1 pound farfalle
2 cups yellow cherry tomatoes
2 cups red cherry tomatoes
Bunch of asparagus, trimmed and sliced
    into 1-inch pieces
12 whole garlic cloves
2 teaspoons sea salt

Juice of 1 lemon (about ¼ cup)
3 tablespoons olive oil
½ cup finely diced red onion
One 8-ounce container 1.5-ounce
    mozzarella balls, cut into eighths
½ cup grated pecorino Romano
¾ cup chopped fresh basil

PREHEAT the oven to 400°F.

BRING a large pot of water to a boil, add the pasta, and cook to your preferred doneness, stirring occasionally. Drain in a colander and rinse with cold water to stop the cooking and set aside in a large bowl.

MEANWHILE, on a large rimmed baking sheet, toss together the tomatoes, asparagus, and garlic. Season with 1 teaspoon of the salt and toss to coat. Roast until the vegetables are soft, about 20 minutes.

REMOVE the garlic cloves to a blender or food processor, add the lemon juice and oil, and puree until smooth.

TRANSFER the remaining roasted vegetables, onion, and mozzarella to the bowl with the pasta. Pour the dressing over the pasta salad, add the pecorino Romano and the remaining teaspoon salt, and toss to coat. Garnish with the basil and serve.

Belizean Black Stew Beans with Coconut Rice

JAZZ: I traveled alone to Belize in my early twenties. After staying in Belize City for one night, I took a long bus trip to a small town where I randomly met another young woman who was traveling alone from England. We were both looking for a hotel and were approached by an older couple who were renting out a room in their house. We rented a room together for ten Belizean dollars each, which at the time was five US dollars a night! Gosh, I know that sounds scary, Mom, but I'm still here.

Anyway, this was one of the best trips ever because I was completely submerged in the culture. If I didn't speak, everyone thought I was a local, and I ate fresh mangoes, pineapples, and watermelon from street vendors all day long. I eventually made it to the tiny island of Caye Caulker, where I rode around on the back of mopeds belonging to friendly locals and then lay in a beach hammock all day with a book.

No matter where I went in the country, they served delicious stewed beans, either black or kidney. They're a staple there, served as a side with breakfast, lunch, and dinner. This is my version. Here's to islands and nomadic travel with abandon!

MAKES 6 TO 8 SERVINGS

STEW BEANS
1 pound dried black beans, sorted and rinsed
½ yellow onion, diced
5 garlic cloves, minced
3 bay leaves
2 teaspoons ground cumin
½ pound bacon, cut crosswise into thin slices
1 tablespoon olive oil
1 teaspoon kosher salt
½ teaspoon ground black pepper
8 whole hot chile peppers

COCONUT RICE
2 cups long-grain white rice
2 tablespoons unrefined coconut oil
½ teaspoon kosher salt
1½ cups coconut milk
1 teaspoon granulated garlic

PLACE the beans in a large stockpot and cover with water. Bring to a boil and cook for 2 minutes. Remove from the heat, cover, and set aside to soak for 1½ hours. Drain the beans and return them to the pot. Cover with 6 cups water, bring to a boil, and cook for 2 minutes. Add the onion, garlic, bay leaves, and cumin. Cover, reduce the heat, and simmer until the beans are tender, about 2 hours. Add the bacon, oil, salt, and pepper and stir to combine. Simmer for 45 minutes more so the flavors can marry.

TO make the coconut rice, place all the ingredients in a medium saucepan with 1½ cups water and stir to combine. Bring to a boil, then reduce the heat, cover, and simmer for 15 to 20 minutes, until the rice is tender. Fluff with a fork.

SERVE the beans with the coconut rice and garnish with the chiles.

Garlic-Mushroom Quinoa

JURNEE: Quinoa has become popular over the past few years as a gluten-free, high-protein alternative to rice and couscous, and this recipe is a favorite for both its flavor and its health benefits. With liquid aminos substituted for soy sauce, you get a protein-rich dish packed with the beneficial amino acids your body will thank you for. You can sauté in a wok for the fried-rice effect or just cook it in a skillet. It's great as a stand-alone dish or as a complement to salmon or another protein.

MAKES 4 MAIN OR 6 SIDE SERVINGS

2 tablespoons sesame oil
1 red onion, finely diced
10 garlic cloves, thinly sliced
2 Fresno chiles, seeded and thinly sliced
6 ounces shiitake or cremini
    mushrooms, thinly sliced

¼ cup sherry or dry white wine
1 cup quinoa, cooked according to the
    package directions
¼ cup liquid aminos
2 tablespoons rice vinegar
Handful of fresh cilantro, chopped
Sriracha, for serving (optional)

HEAT the oil over high heat in a large wok or heavy-bottomed skillet. When the oil is almost smoking, add the onion, garlic, and chiles. Stirring the vegetables quickly so they don't burn, cook until soft, 4 to 5 minutes. Add the mushrooms, stir, and cook for 1 minute. Deglaze the pan with the sherry and cook until the sherry reduces by about half, about 1 minute. Add the cooked quinoa, liquid aminos, and vinegar, stir, and cook until all the liquid is absorbed, about 1 minute. Turn off the heat, toss in the cilantro, and serve immediately! Drizzle with a little sriracha, if desired.

Creamed Spinach

This family favorite belongs in some great American steakhouse somewhere. Lighter than most creamed spinach, it has that classic taste without drowning out the taste of the greens.

MAKES 4 TO 6 SERVINGS

6 tablespoons salted butter
4 garlic cloves, finely minced
2 tablespoons minced yellow onion
¼ teaspoon sea salt
½ teaspoon ground white pepper
1½ cups heavy cream

⅔ cup grated Parmesan, plus more for serving
Two 10-ounce boxes chopped frozen spinach, thawed, excess water squeezed out

MELT the butter in a large skillet over medium heat. Add the garlic and onion and cook, stirring often, until they are crisp and deep brown (but not burned), 4 to 5 minutes. Season with the salt and the pepper and add the cream. Bring to a boil, then reduce the heat to a rolling simmer, and cook until the cream reduces by a third and thickens slightly. Add the Parmesan and let the cheese melt into the cream. Fold in the spinach and cook for 3 minutes, until warmed through and well incorporated. Top with more grated cheese, and serve.

Cajun Fries

JAKE: I love battered fries, especially when they are extra crispy with cajun spices.   MAKES 4 SERVINGS

FAT FRIES
½ cup white rice flour
1 cup buttermilk
4 large russet potatoes, scrubbed and
     cut into French fries (about 25 fries
     per potato)
Vegetable oil, for frying

SEASONING MIX
1½ teaspoons granulated onion
1½ teaspoons granulated garlic
1 teaspoon smoked paprika
¼ teaspoon cayenne pepper
¼ teaspoon ground white pepper
1½ teaspoons sea salt

DIPPING SAUCE
¼ cup mayonnaise
2 tablespoons ketchup
1½ teaspoons hot sauce

WHISK together the flour and buttermilk in a large bowl. Toss the potatoes in the mixture to coat them well.

COMBINE the seasoning mix ingredients in another large bowl.

LINE a baking sheet with paper towels and set aside. Heat 2 inches oil in a large cast-iron skillet or heavy-bottomed frying pan over high heat until very hot. (Dip a fry in the oil and if it sizzles, the oil is ready.)

Working in batches so as not to overcrowd the pan, fry the potatoes until they are deep golden brown, about 6 minutes. Remove the fries with a slotted spoon or spatula to the lined baking sheet to absorb the excess oil, then immediately toss them in the spice mixture.

WHISK together the dipping sauce ingredients in a small bowl and serve with the fries.

Crabmeat Potatoes au Gratin

JAKE: Potatoes au gratin originated in France in the seventeenth century, and this deliciously cheesy delight has been feeding our family for as long as we can remember. The elegant simplicity of the dish gives it room for reinvention, letting families put their own spin on it while still sharing a culinary tradition. Our family created a Cajun interpretation of the French classic, with fresh lumps of crabmeat adding a fresh, tangy pop of flavor against the creamy backdrop of perfectly blended cheese. Enjoy with your very best of friends!

MAKES 8 TO 10 SERVINGS

---

2 tablespoons salted butter, plus more for greasing

1 pound fresh jumbo lump crabmeat, drained

9 garlic cloves, minced

1 tablespoon sea salt

½ teaspoon ground black pepper

3 pounds red potatoes, scrubbed and cut into ¼-inch slices (about 7 large potatoes)

½ cup finely sliced green onions

6 cups grated Monterey Jack (about 1½ pounds)

1 cup heavy cream

PREHEAT the oven to 350°F. Grease a 9 × 13-inch baking dish with butter and set aside.

MELT the butter over high heat in a medium skillet. Add the crab and all but 1 teaspoon of the garlic and sauté until the garlic is fragrant, about 2 minutes. Remove from the heat.

MIX together the reserved garlic and the salt and pepper.

TO assemble the gratin, arrange an even layer of potatoes in the baking dish. Top evenly with ½ teaspoon of the garlic-salt mix, 1½ tablespoons of the green onion, 1 cup of the crab mixture, and 1½ cups of the cheese. Repeat the layers twice more, then do a final layer of just potatoes, garlic-salt mix, green onions, and cheese—no crab. Pour the heavy cream around the edges of the pan and cover it tightly with foil.

BAKE for 1 hour 15 minutes, uncover, and bake for 20 minutes more, until the top layer is golden and gooey.

Chicken Curry Rice

JAKE: This dish is so quick and simple to make but is packed with flavor. On my trip to Jamaica with my brothers, I loved watching the chefs work their magic with a variety of different curries. This is one of my favorite simple curry dishes.

MAKES 8 TO 10 SERVINGS

½ pound boneless, skinless chicken breast, thinly sliced
Sea salt
2 tablespoons olive oil
1 yellow onion, halved and thinly sliced
2½ teaspoons granulated garlic
1 tablespoon ground turmeric

2½ tablespoons mild yellow curry powder
1 teaspoon ground coriander
½ teaspoon cayenne pepper
2-inch fresh ginger knob, peeled and halved
1 cup frozen peas
6 cups cooked brown basmati rice

SEASON the chicken with 1 teaspoon salt. Heat the oil over medium heat in a large high-sided sauté pan. Add the chicken, onion, granulated garlic, turmeric, curry powder, coriander, cayenne, ginger halves, and 1½ teaspoons salt and sauté, stirring often, until the chicken is cooked through, 6 minutes. Add the peas and cook until they defrost, 3 to 5 minutes. Add the rice and fold the mixture together. As soon as the rice is warmed through, remove from the heat and serve.

Cheesy Broccoli

JURNEE: Wherever we lived, we always had a revolving door of neighborhood kids who would just invite themselves into our house and open the fridge or hang out in the kitchen. This particular dish usually earned us friends! Broccoli and cheese is often a childhood favorite, and our irresistible cheese sauce made ours even more of a draw. You'll be hooked on this simple side dish!

MAKES 4 TO 6 SERVINGS

---

7 cups broccoli florets (from about 3 heads)
1 tablespoon olive oil
¼ teaspoon sea salt
½ teaspoon granulated garlic

1 cup grated Fontina (about 4 ounces)
1½ cups grated white sharp Cheddar (about 6 ounces)
3 tablespoons panko bread crumbs
2 tablespoons salted butter, melted

PREHEAT the oven to 400°F.

PLACE the broccoli and ½ cup water in a large stockpot over high heat. Bring to a boil, then reduce the heat, cover, and simmer until the broccoli is knife tender and steamed through, about 10 minutes. Stir in the oil, salt, and granulated garlic. Add the Fontina and 1 cup of the Cheddar and stir, cooking until it melts completely, about 2 minutes.

Transfer the mixture to a 9 × 13-inch baking dish. Top the broccoli with the remaining ½ cup Cheddar.

USING a fork, mix together in a small bowl the panko and butter until combined. Sprinkle the panko over the cheese and bake until the cheese is gooey and the panko has turned golden brown, about 30 minutes. Serve immediately.

Crabby Fried Rice

JAKE: This crab fried rice is all I need in one dish. It's light with the brown rice and crab, but the pickled ginger and crispy garlic set it off for me.

MAKES 6 TO 8 SERVINGS

---

2 tablespoons salted butter

2 tablespoons toasted sesame oil

8 garlic cloves, minced

1 tablespoon grated peeled fresh ginger

1 pound fresh jumbo lump crabmeat, drained

2 tablespoons rice vinegar

¼ cup plus 1 tablespoon low-sodium soy sauce

½ red onion, thinly sliced

¼ orange bell pepper, cored, seeded, and finely diced

¼ red bell pepper, cored, seeded, and finely diced

½ cup roasted unsalted cashews

2 cups jasmine rice, cooked according to the package directions

One 8-ounce can pineapple chunks, drained

Handful of fresh cilantro, chopped

MELT the butter in the oil in a medium cast-iron skillet over high heat. Add the garlic and ginger and sauté until fragrant and golden, about 2 minutes. Add the crab and toss to combine. Season the crab with the vinegar and the ¼ cup soy sauce, then add the onion, bell peppers, and cashews and cook until the onions and peppers are slightly softened, about 5 minutes. Add the rice and toss to incorporate. Remove from the heat and fold in the pineapple and remaining soy sauce. Garnish with the cilantro and serve.

Dill Potato Salad

JURNEE: Every Thanksgiving, we all show up and show out. This here is one of my specialties, a twist on classic potato salad, which is always in high demand at the Thanksgiving table but perfect year-round. The secret is in the spicy brown mustard, which gives the potatoes a nice kick. Enjoy!

MAKES 6 TO 8 SERVINGS

---

4 large russet potatoes
1 cup finely diced celery (about 2 large stalks)
1 cup finely diced yellow onion (about ½ large onion)
1 cup mayonnaise

½ cup spicy brown mustard
½ cup dill relish
1 teaspoon sea salt
½ teaspoon cayenne pepper
1 teaspoon dried dill
Handful of fresh dill, chopped

PLACE the potatoes in a large pot and cover them with water. Bring to a boil, then reduce the heat and simmer for about 1 hour, until knife tender. Drain the potatoes and set them aside. When cool enough to handle, pull the peels off the potatoes with your fingers or a knife and discard.

Roughly chop the potatoes and transfer them to a large bowl. Add the celery, onion, mayonnaise, mustard, relish, salt, cayenne, and dried dill and gently stir to combine well.

TRANSFER to a serving dish and garnish with the fresh dill.

PARTY
Bites & Snacks

JAZZ: Our family has always tried to find any excuse to throw a party or gathering. We love the communal joy of sharing food, laughs, and love around a celebration. Whether it's a small birthday party, an at-home movie night, or a larger gathering of friends and extended family, we always enjoy these moments around good food and good company.

When we were very young, living in Northern California, on Friday evenings our parents' friends and their kids would all gather at our house. Their friends consisted of local musicians, artists, and activists. Guests arrived with instruments for pop-up jam sessions, record albums for games of "Name That Tune," and snacks or drinks to contribute to the celebration. Our parents prepared a few small dishes and bowls of snacks. Mom drank sparkling water from a wineglass, and Dad and their friends drank beer from the bottle. Dad wore T-shirts and dungarees and played the mandolin, while Mom—with bells on her skirt and fringe on her boots—was always the life of the party. We'd eat too much and run around with the other kids until we could no longer keep ourselves awake. We'd often fall asleep as the music played into the night.

These dishes are the "little something extra" that work perfectly as party appetizers, everyday snacks, or with the right combination, a tapas-style meal that combines a variety of flavors to satisfy any palate. We hope you enjoy abundantly!

Crispy Beef-Lettuce Wraps

JAKE: Japanese food is one of my favorites cuisines, and anytime I get to eat it I'm happy. These crispy steak-lettuce cups are fresh and hearty and are Japanese inspired. Thinly sliced cuts of steak are deep fried and coated in a velvety brown sauce with rich umami flavor. **MAKES 6 SERVINGS**

GARLIC-GINGER SAUCE
2 tablespoons toasted sesame oil
2 tablespoons liquid aminos
¼ cup rice vinegar
2 garlic cloves, pressed
½ teaspoon grated peeled fresh ginger
1 teaspoon honey

CARROT-GINGER SAUCE
1 medium carrot, chopped (about ½ cup)
¼ cup toasted sesame oil
2 tablespoons plus ½ teaspoon apple cider vinegar
½ teaspoon grated peeled fresh ginger
1 garlic clove, smashed
½ teaspoon kosher salt

PICKLED ONIONS
½ red onion, thinly sliced
½ cup rice wine vinegar

BEEF
1 pound top sirloin steak, cut against the grain into ⅛-inch slices
1 tablespoon liquid aminos
1 tablespoon granulated garlic
1 cup cornstarch
2 cups canola oil

TO ASSEMBLE
Head of Bibb lettuce, leaves separated
2 Hass avocados, pitted, peeled, and thinly sliced
Handful of fresh cilantro

TO make the garlic-ginger sauce, combine all the ingredients in a small saucepan over medium heat. Bring to a simmer and cook for 2 minutes, until the mixture bubbles. Remove from the heat and set aside so the flavors can mingle.

TO make the carrot-ginger sauce, puree all the ingredients in a food processor until smooth. Transfer to a medium bowl and set aside.

TO make the pickled onions, combine the onion and vinegar in a medium bowl, making sure the onion slices are submerged in the vinegar. Refrigerate for 10 to 15 minutes. These will keep in an airtight container in the fridge for up to 2 weeks.

TO make the beef, place the steak in a medium bowl, season with the liquid aminos and granulated garlic, and toss with the cornstarch. (You can also combine the ingredients in a zip-top bag.)

LINE a baking sheet with paper towels. Heat the canola oil in a wok or large high-sided

sauté pan over high heat until the oil is almost smoking. Working in batches so as not to overcrowd the pan, fry the beef until golden brown and crispy, 4 minutes total. Remove the beef to the lined baking sheet to absorb the excess oil, then transfer to a large bowl.

REHEAT the garlic-ginger sauce, add it to the bowl with the beef, and toss to coat.

TO build your lettuce wrap, first add the beef, avocado, and pickled onions, then drizzle the carrot-ginger dressing on top and sprinkle with cilantro.

PARTY BITES & SNACKS

161

Eggplant Parm Pizza Rounds

JAKE: We ate eggplant Parmesan regularly growing up, and it's the inspiration for these pizza-like eggplant Parmesan rounds. The eggplant is sliced into thin rounds, fried crispy, and layered with sauce and cheese on top. It's a really cool way to serve eggplant Parm in appetizer form. I love these little guys.

MAKES 16 ROUNDS, TO SERVE 4 TO 6

EGGPLANT ROUNDS
1 large eggplant
Vegetable oil, for frying
1 cup grated Parmesan (about 4 ounces)
1 Roma tomato, cut into 16 thin slices
Large handful of fresh basil leaves,
    thinly sliced

DRY BATTER
1 cup unbleached all-purpose flour
1 cup processed grated Parmesan, such
    as Kraft
½ tablespoon dried basil

1 teaspoon crushed red pepper
½ teaspoon kosher salt

EGG BATTER
3 eggs
1 teaspoon sea salt
½ teaspoon ground black pepper

TOMATO SAUCE
4 garlic cloves, chopped
2 tablespoons olive oil
1 cup tomato paste
½ teaspoon sea salt
1 teaspoon crushed red pepper

WITH a sharp serrated knife, trim the eggplant and cut it into ¼-inch rounds. You'll get about 16 slices out of a large eggplant.

COMBINE all the dry batter ingredients in a large bowl. Lightly whisk together the egg batter ingredients in a medium bowl. One at a time, dip the eggplant rounds into the egg batter, then the dry batter. Make sure the eggplant is completely coated in the dry batter, pressing it into the eggplant to ensure a nice coating for frying. (This step could be done the day before if needed. After dredging your eggplant, place it on a baking sheet and wrap in plastic. Store

in the fridge until ready to fry. This may increase the frying time slightly.)

LINE a plate with paper towels and set aside. Heat ⅛ inch vegetable oil in a large cast-iron skillet or heavy-bottomed frying pan over high heat until very hot. (Dip the edge of an eggplant round in the oil and if it sizzles, the oil is ready.) Working in batches so as not to overcrowd the skillet, fry the eggplant rounds for 3 minutes per side, or until crispy and golden brown. Remove the rounds to the lined plate to absorb the excess oil.

PREHEAT the oven to 425°F.

TO make the tomato sauce, sauté the garlic in the olive oil in a medium saucepan over medium-high heat until softened, about 1 minute. Add the tomato paste, salt, crushed red pepper, and ⅓ cup water, stir, and cook for about 5 minutes. Remove from the heat.

LINE two rimmed baking sheets with parchment paper and divide the rounds between them. Top the rounds with sauce, Parmesan, a thin slice of fresh tomato, and basil. Bake for about 5 minutes, until the cheese is melted.

Spicy Fish Cakes

JAKE: If you like crab cakes, these fish cakes are the same idea—shredded fish formed into a two-bite appetizer. I love when fish is told in a different way, and these will have everybody asking for more.

MAKES 16 FISH CAKES

FISH CAKES

1 pound very finely minced white fish, such as snapper or trout

¼ cup plus 2 teaspoons toasted sesame oil

4 garlic cloves, chopped

3 green onions, minced, white and light green parts separated

1½ tablespoons liquid aminos

1 tablespoon sriracha

1 teaspoon granulated onion

1 teaspoon granulated garlic

1 large egg

½ cup panko bread crumbs

Chopped fresh flat-leaf parsley

Lemon wedges, for serving

DIPPING SAUCE

2 tablespoons mayonnaise

2 tablespoons sweet relish

1 tablespoon sriracha

TO make the fish cakes, place the minced fish in a large bowl, using paper towels to soak up any excess liquid from the fish if necessary. Add the 2 teaspoons oil to a small sauté pan over medium heat. Add the garlic and cook until soft, about 2 minutes. Pour the oil and garlic into the bowl of fish. Add the white parts of the green onion, the liquid aminos, sriracha, granulated onion, granulated garlic, egg, and panko and mix gently to combine well.

FOR each fish cake, spoon out about 1½ tablespoons of the mixture and form it into a ball with your hands, then flatten it to your desired thickness (I prefer them on the thin side).

LINE a plate with paper towels and set aside. Heat the remaining ¼ cup oil in a large nonstick sauté pan over medium heat. Working in batches so as not to overcrowd the pan, fry the fish cakes for about 3 minutes per side, or until golden brown. As you finish frying, remove the fish cakes to the lined plate to absorb the excess oil.

TO make the dipping sauce, combine the mayonnaise, relish, and sriracha in a small bowl.

GARNISH the fish cakes with the parsley and serve them with lemon wedges and dipping sauce on the side. They're great as a stand-alone appetizer but also go well with a green salad or quinoa. Enjoy!

Loaded Turkey Burger Sliders

JAKE: It's funny how the turkey burger phenomenon just took over in my family. I remember when everything was beef, then one day in the mid-1990s we went into Costco and saw these giant packs of ground turkey, and Mom never looked back.

These sliders stand up and show out. The taste of bacon, jalapeño, onion, garlic, mushrooms, and cheese in every bite makes me weak. I'm a sucker for a good burger.

MAKES 12 SLIDERS

8 slices thick-cut bacon
½ small yellow onion, finely chopped
2 garlic cloves, minced
2 baby bella mushrooms, finely chopped
¼ jalapeño chile, seeded and minced
1 pound ground turkey
2 tablespoons Worcestershire sauce
¼ teaspoon sea salt
¼ teaspoon paprika
¼ cup grated smoked Gouda

12 brioche slider buns
¼ cup grated Parmesan
1 jalapeño chile, cut into 12 slices

SRIRACHA MAYO
¼ cup mayonnaise
2 tablespoons sriracha, or to taste

SPECIAL EQUIPMENT: 12 short knotted skewers

LINE a plate with paper towels and set aside. Arrange the bacon in a large cast-iron skillet or heavy-bottomed frying pan over high heat and cook until crispy, 3 to 4 minutes on each side. Remove the bacon to the lined plate to absorb the excess oil. Reserve 1 tablespoon of the bacon grease in the skillet.

RETURN the skillet to medium-high heat, add the onion, garlic, mushrooms, and minced jalapeño. Sauté until the vegetables are soft, about 5 minutes.

PLACE the turkey in a large bowl and top with the cooked veggies. Chop half of the bacon into small pieces. Cut the remaining slices into 3 pieces each and set aside. Add the chopped bacon to the bowl and mix to combine. Add the Worcestershire, salt, paprika, and Gouda and mix until combined.

USE your hands to divide the meat into 12 equal patties. Pat them to about 3 inches wide to fit on the slider buns.

WHISK together the mayonnaise and sriracha in a small bowl and set aside.

HEAT a large cast-iron skillet over medium-high heat. Working in batches so as not to overcrowd the skillet, cook the patties 5 to 7 minutes per side, until browned throughout and slightly crispy. Remove to a plate. Open the slider buns and toast them in the same skillet.

TO assemble the sliders, spread some sriracha mayonnaise on both halves of the buns, add a patty, and sprinkle a little grated Parmesan on top. Add the top bun and skewer the slider with a piece of bacon and a jalapeño slice. So good!

Mini Croque-Monsieurs

JAZZ: These cute, gooey little French sandwiches are so fun to eat and are a hit every time we serve them at a party. The secret is the Mornay sauce, which pulls the flavors together beautifully and makes these irresistible little snacks something to write home about! **MAKES 12 APPETIZERS**

One 10-ounce French baguette, cut into twenty-four ¼-inch slices
¼ cup mayonnaise
¼ cup country-style Dijon mustard
6 slices Black Forest ham
3 tablespoons unsalted butter

¼ cup unbleached all-purpose flour
1 cup whole milk
¼ teaspoon kosher salt
⅛ teaspoon ground nutmeg
1½ cups grated Gruyère (about 6 ounces)

ARRANGE the bread slices on a baking sheet and spread each one with ½ teaspoon mayonnaise.

HEAT a large skillet over medium-high heat. Place the bread slices, mayonnaise side down, in the skillet and toast until browned, about 3 minutes. Return 12 of the toasted bread slices to the baking sheet, toasted side down, and spread 1 teaspoon mustard on each untoasted side.

FOLD each slice of ham into thirds, as if folding a letter, then cut it in half crosswise to yield 12 total pieces. Place the ham squares on top of the mustard.

PREHEAT the broiler to high.

MELT the butter in a medium saucepan over medium heat. Whisk in the flour to combine and cook until light brown, 1 to 2 minutes. Whisking constantly, slowly add the milk and cook until the sauce thickens, about 3 minutes. Whisk in the salt and nutmeg. Add 1 cup of the Gruyère and whisk until the cheese is melted and the sauce is smooth, about 1 minute. Remove the Mornay sauce from the heat, spoon 1 tablespoon over each square of ham, and top with 1 teaspoon of the remaining Gruyère.

BROIL for 1 minute, or until the cheese is melted, watching carefully so that the sandwiches don't burn. Top each sandwich with a slice of the remaining toasted bread. Serve the sandwiches warm.

Togarashi Onion Rings with Wasabi Dipping Sauce

JAZZ: These onion rings have a double inspiration, from the Texas steakhouses we've eaten at while visiting family there and from our countless visits to Japanese restaurants in California. These flavors are so rich that they stand on their own as a tapas snack at a party or as a side dish to a burger or steak. Extremely versatile!

MAKES 4 TO 6 SIDE SERVINGS

WASABI DIPPING SAUCE

1 cup mayonnaise

¼ cup rice wine vinegar

2 teaspoons sugar

1 teaspoon wasabi paste

2 teaspoons togarashi powder, plus more for sprinkling

ONION RINGS

Vegetable oil, for frying

2 cups buttermilk

4 cups panko bread crumbs

2 cups unbleached all-purpose flour

¼ cup black toasted sesame seeds

4 teaspoons cayenne pepper

4 teaspoons granulated garlic

4 teaspoons granulated onion

4 teaspoons kosher salt

2 large yellow onions, cut crosswise into ½-inch slices

¼ cup pickled ginger, julienned, for serving

SPECIAL EQUIPMENT: deep-fry thermometer

WHISK together the mayonnaise, vinegar, sugar, wasabi, and the 2 teaspoons togarashi in a medium bowl. Refrigerate until ready to serve.

HEAT 3 inches oil in a large Dutch oven to 365°F.

SET up a dredging station with two shallow dishes, one with the buttermilk and one with the panko, flour, sesame seeds, cayenne, granulated garlic, granulated onion, and salt. Lightly whisk together the dry ingredients.

SEPARATE the onion slices into rings. Dip each ring in the buttermilk and then in the seasoned panko mixture. Set the rings in a single layer on a baking sheet as you finish dredging the rest.

LINE a plate with paper towels and set aside. Working in batches so as not to overcrowd the Dutch oven, fry the breaded onion rings until golden brown and crispy, about 4 minutes, flipping them over halfway through. Remove the onion rings to the lined plate and season with more togarashi. Serve the onion rings with the wasabi dipping sauce and pickled ginger.

GRAPEFRUIT-LIME VODKA

Juice of 1 small grapefruit (about ¾ cup)
Juice of 2 limes (about ¼ cup)
¼ cup vodka

1½ teaspoons simple syrup
(see page 223)
1 mint sprig

Mix together the grapefruit and lime juices, vodka, and simple syrup in a shaker. Pour over ice and garnish with the mint! MAKES 1 DRINK

Fried Shrimp Hand Rolls

JAKE: Here in Los Angeles a lot of people (myself included) believe that sushi in SoCal is second only to that in Tokyo. I love a hand roll bar here called KazuNori. They deliver patrons the best, freshest hand rolls made with sushi rice, crunchy nori, and everything from yellowtail to lobster. One day I decided to try my own take on them, so I fried some shrimp and tossed them in an epic garlic-soy-ginger sauce and threw them in a hand roll. Magic, I tell you! Magic!

MAKES 12 ROLLS

SUSHI RICE
2 cups short-grain sushi rice, such as Shirakiku rice

2 tablespoons unseasoned rice vinegar

1 tablespoon sugar

1 teaspoon sea salt

SHRIMP
1 pound medium shrimp, peeled and deveined, tails removed, halved lengthwise (butterfly the shrimp but cut all the way through)

Zest of 1 lemon

2 teaspoons dried minced onion

1½ tablespoons low-sodium soy sauce

½ teaspoon crushed red pepper

1 teaspoon sambal

½ cup white rice flour

¼ cup unbleached all-purpose flour

Vegetable oil, for frying

SAUCE
1 tablespoon toasted sesame oil

2 tablespoons low-sodium soy sauce

2 tablespoons unseasoned rice vinegar

3 garlic cloves, pressed

NORI AND ACCOMPANIMENTS
12 toasted nori seaweed sheets

1 bunch green onions, thinly sliced

Wasabi paste

Pickled ginger

Soy sauce

TO make the sushi rice, combine the rice and 2¾ cups water in a medium saucepan and stir in the vinegar, sugar, and salt to incorporate. Bring to a boil, uncovered, then reduce the heat to low and cover. Let the rice cook for about 15 minutes, or until the water has evaporated. Set aside off the heat.

PLACE the shrimp in a medium bowl and stir in the lemon zest, onion, soy sauce, crushed red pepper, and sambal. Whisk together the flours in a small bowl, then add the mixture

to the seasoned shrimp and toss to coat every piece evenly.

LINE a plate with paper towels and set aside. Heat 1 inch of oil in a large cast-iron skillet or heavy-bottomed saucepan over high heat until very hot. (Drop a little of the batter in the oil and if it sizzles, the oil is ready.) Place the shrimp on a baking sheet (this will make it easier to quickly transfer them to the skillet). Working in batches so as not to overcrowd the pan, fry the shrimp for

about 3 to 5 minutes, until crispy and golden brown. Remove the shrimp to the lined plate to absorb the excess oil.

TO make the sauce, whisk together all the ingredients in a large bowl until smooth. Transfer the hot shrimp to the bowl and toss to coat the shrimp in that delicious sauce.

TO make a single hand roll, lay a sheet of nori and spread 2 tablespoons of rice in a strip across the end of the sheet. Place 3 or 4 shrimp over the rice and top it with about 1 teaspoon sliced green onions. Roll the hand roll like a burrito from the rice end down until it's fully closed, leaving the top and bottom exposed. Continue making rolls until all the shrimp has been used up.

SERVE immediately with the wasabi, pickled ginger, and soy sauce. Enjoy!

Corn–Cauliflower Chowder

JAZZ: This soup is so warm and creamy. The corn adds a hint of sweetness and solidifies this dish as an elevated comfort food. Try this with a baguette and serve as an appetizer at your next dinner party!

MAKES 4 APPETIZERS

Head of cauliflower, broken into florets (about 4 cups)
One 16-ounce bag frozen sweet corn
6 garlic cloves, minced
4 tablespoons (½ stick) salted butter or ¼ cup olive oil for a vegan dish

Pinch of cayenne pepper
½ teaspoon pink Himalayan salt
1½ cups vegetable stock
Extra-virgin olive oil

PLACE the cauliflower, corn, garlic, and ½ cup water in a medium saucepan, cover, and bring to a boil, 2 to 3 minutes. Reduce the heat and simmer, covered, until the cauliflower is steamed through and soft, about 25 minutes. Add the butter or olive oil, cayenne, and salt and stir to help the butter melt.

TRANSFER the mixture to a blender, add the stock, and puree until completely smooth. Use caution as the liquid will still be hot. Pour the chowder into serving bowls and drizzle with a little olive oil. Serve hot!

Asian Lobster Wonton Tacos

JUSSIE: I didn't like lobster when I was growing up in New York City. I felt like it was reserved for rich businessmen on Wall Street or for Mommy, when she'd have a fancy craving after giving birth for the ninetieth time. It was in the same category as caviar and limos, two other things I had no interest in. Plus I'm a lazy eater; I don't like to work when I eat, so all that cracking of the shell and *blah blah blah* was not amusing.

Now that I'm older? I literally look for excuses to put lobster in dishes. You want an omelet? Put some lobster in it! *Yooooo*, you're making fried chicken? Fry that lobster instead! So these lobster tacos win me over every single time.

MAKES 12 MINI TACOS, TO SERVE 4 TO 6

---

1 teaspoon toasted sesame oil
2 teaspoons fresh lemon juice
¼ teaspoon grated peeled fresh ginger
3 tablespoons low-sodium soy sauce
5 garlic cloves, minced
1 cup thinly sliced green cabbage (about ¼ small cabbage)
1 cup thinly sliced red cabbage (about ¼ small cabbage)

1½ cups vegetable oil
12 wonton wrappers
4 tablespoons (½ stick) unsalted butter
4 green onions, thinly sliced
Six 5-ounce lobster tails, meat removed from the shell and cut into 1-inch dice
Sriracha (optional)

COMBINE the sesame oil, lemon juice, ginger, 1 tablespoon of the soy sauce, and 1 teaspoon of the minced garlic in a large bowl. Add the green and red cabbage, toss to coat, and set aside.

LINE a plate with paper towels and set aside. Heat the vegetable oil in a small saucepan over medium heat. Fold 12 wonton wrappers in half into the shape of hard taco shells. Using tongs to hold the edge of the wrapper and a slotted spatula in the middle of the wrapper to make the taco shell shape, fry the wrappers one at a time until crunchy, about 30 seconds per side. Remove the wonton shells to the lined plate to absorb the excess oil and set aside.

MELT the butter in a medium sauté pan over medium heat. Add the remaining garlic and sauté about 1 minute, until softened. Add the green onions, the remaining 2 tablespoons soy sauce, and the lobster and sauté until the meat is cooked through, 2 to 3 minutes.

DIVIDE the lobster among the fried wonton shells, top these mini tacos with cabbage slaw, and drizzle them with sriracha to taste if desired. Serve immediately.

THE FAMILY TABLE

Potato Knishes

JURNEE: One of the best things about growing up in New York was the street vendors. On any corner you could find abundant food options, like my favorite New York street vendor and deli snack, the potato knish. I remember trying it for the first time on Coney Island. There's nothing like biting into the soft mashed potatoes wrapped in the crispy crust with a dollop of mustard on top! This is our version of one of our favorites!

MAKES ABOUT 12 KNISHES

DOUGH
4 cups unbleached all-purpose flour, plus more for rolling out the dough
1 teaspoon baking powder
1 teaspoon kosher salt
½ teaspoon granulated onion
½ teaspoon granulated garlic
1 large egg
½ cup buttermilk
½ cup vegetable oil

FILLING
2 pounds russet potatoes (about 2 large potatoes)

4 tablespoons (½ stick) salted butter
1 small yellow onion, halved and thinly sliced
3 large garlic cloves, minced
½ cup buttermilk
1½ teaspoons kosher salt
½ teaspoon ground black pepper

2 egg yolks, lightly whisked

FOR SERVING
Sour cream
1 bunch green onions, thinly sliced
Spicy brown mustard

TO make the dough, pulse 3 cups of the flour, the baking powder, salt, granulated onion, and granulated garlic in a food processor until just combined. Turn off the machine and add the egg, buttermilk, and oil. Pulse the ingredients together until completely combined and then, with the motor running, stream in ¼ cup cold water until the dough forms a ball. Remove the dough, wrap it tightly in plastic wrap, and refrigerate it at least 1 hour before using.

PLACE a rack in the center of the oven and preheat the oven to 375°F. Line two baking sheets with parchment paper.

PLACE the potatoes in a medium saucepan and cover them with cold water. Bring the water to a boil, then reduce the heat and simmer for about 1 hour, until knife tender. Drain the potatoes and set them aside to cool slightly.

WHILE the potatoes are cooking, melt the butter in a medium sauté pan over medium heat. Add the onion slices and cook until lightly caramelized, about 25 minutes, stirring occasionally so they don't burn. Reduce the heat to low, add the garlic, and cook about 5 minutes, until the garlic is soft and the onion slices are evenly caramelized. Set aside to cool completely.

PEEL the potatoes and place them in the food processor. Add the buttermilk, salt, and pepper and pulse until the mixture is just smooth; do not overmix or the mixture will become gummy. Remove the mixture from the food processor to a medium bowl, stir in the caramelized onions, and set the filling aside.

REMOVE the dough from the fridge. It will feel a bit oily; this is normal. Generously dust a clean work surface and your hands with flour and cut the dough in half. Roll the dough into a 12 × 16-inch rectangle. Cut the dough width-wise into three 4-inch strips, and then cut the strips in half crosswise. This will give you six 4 × 8-inch rectangles. Repeat with the second half of the dough.

PLACE 3 tablespoons of the filling in the center of a dough rectangle and brush the edges of the dough with the egg yolk. Fold the dough over the filling to make a 4 × 4-inch square, then firmly press the edges of the knish together to seal completely, taking care to push out any excess air from around the filling. Poke a small hole on the top of the knish to create a vent, then set 6 knishes on each lined baking sheet. Form the remaining knishes, then brush the tops of all the knishes with more egg wash.

BAKE until lightly golden brown, about 20 minutes. Set aside to cool for 10 minutes before serving.

SERVE the knishes with sour cream, green onions, and spicy brown mustard.

Fajita Chorizo Mexican Pizzas

JURNEE: This is one of those dishes that's impressive with barely any effort. Your family and friends may say, "What in the world? . . . This is sooo good!" You'll then smile and graciously say, "Why, thank you, it's just a little chorizo, onions, peppers, and cheese. Can't go wrong there!" MAKES 12 MINI PIZZAS

ENCHILADA SAUCE
4 dried ancho chiles
2 garlic cloves
½ small onion, roughly chopped
1 Roma tomato, roughly chopped
½ tablespoon fresh oregano
1½ teaspoons sea salt

PIZZA
3 Mexican chorizo sausage links, casings removed

1 small red onion, halved top to bottom and thinly sliced
4 assorted mini–bell peppers, cored, seeded, and cut into ¼-inch rounds
Twelve 4-inch flour tortillas
2 cups shredded Monterey Jack (about 8 ounces)
Handful of fresh cilantro, chopped

PLACE two racks in the center of the oven and preheat the oven to 400°F. Line two baking sheets with foil.

TO make the enchilada sauce, combine the anchos, garlic, onion, tomato, and oregano in a medium saucepan over high heat. Add water to cover and bring to a boil, then reduce the heat and simmer for 20 minutes, until all the vegetables have softened. Remove from heat. Allow to cool for 10 minutes uncovered. Transfer the solids to a blender and puree, adding some of the cooking liquid a little at a time, using up to ¾ cup, until the sauce is smooth. Add the salt and stir.

HEAT a large skillet over high heat, add the chorizo, and cook until browned, 5 to 7 minutes, breaking it up with a wooden

spoon. Remove the chorizo to a plate. Add the onions and peppers to the skillet and cook until softened, 3 to 5 minutes.

TO assemble the pizzas, divide the tortillas between the lined baking sheets and spread each with about ¼ cup of the enchilada sauce. Divide the chorizo, peppers, and onions evenly over the sauce and top with the cheese.

SET the baking sheets on the two different oven racks and bake until the cheese is melted and the tortillas begin to brown around the edges, about 10 minutes, rotating the pans halfway through. Cut each pizza into 4 wedges so that each piece is about the size of a tortilla chip, garnish with the cilantro, and serve immediately.

HORCHATA COCKTAIL

1 cinnamon stick, preferably Mexican
1 vanilla bean, split
1¼ cups sugar
2 cups horchata

Juice of 4 limes (about ½ cup)
½ cup mezcal
½ teaspoon ground cinnamon
Lime wedges

BRING to a boil 1 cup water, the cinnamon stick, vanilla bean, and 1 cup of the sugar in a small saucepan over medium heat. Reduce the heat and simmer until the sugar is dissolved, 5 to 8 minutes. Turn off the heat and let cool to room temperature, about 10 minutes.

WHEN the simple syrup is cool, pour it into a large pitcher and add the horchata, lime juice, and mezcal. Stir to combine.

COMBINE the remaining ¼ cup sugar and the ground cinnamon in a small shallow dish. Dip the rims of cocktail glasses into the horchata cocktail mixture, then into the cinnamon sugar. Add ice to the sugar-rimmed glasses. Pour in the horchata cocktail and garnish with lime wedges. Drink up! MAKES ABOUT 1 QUART

Pork Pot Stickers

JAKE: Growing up, I was pot sticker boy, churning out hundreds of pork pot stickers for my family, starting around age ten. This involved grinding up pounds of pork; seasoning it with garlic, soy sauce, and other flavorings; placing a spoonful on a small wonton skin; sealing it; and deep-frying it to perfection. It can be a tedious process, but it's so worth it. Sometimes I'd be making a ton of these and find a crowd of siblings standing near the fryer waiting for them to emerge. I still had more pot stickers to fry, of course, so they'd go off and enjoy them, leaving me with a few stragglers. Oh, being the fifth of six kids. The war stories I have of fighting for food will leave you pitying me, but that's another book— or a therapy session.

MAKES 30 POT STICKERS

POT STICKERS
2 pounds ground pork
4 green onions, minced
2 tablespoons toasted sesame oil
6 tablespoons low-sodium soy sauce
2 teaspoons grated peeled fresh ginger
2 teaspoons granulated onion
2 teaspoons granulated garlic

½ teaspoon sea salt
30 wonton wrappers
Vegetable oil, for frying

DIPPING SAUCE
⅔ cup low-sodium soy sauce
½ cup rice vinegar
4 teaspoons crushed red pepper

USING your hands or a wooden spoon, in a large bowl mix together the pork, green onions, oil, soy sauce, ginger, granulated onion, granulated garlic, and salt until fully incorporated.

LAY out the wonton wrappers and spoon 1 tablespoon of the pork filling into the center of each square. Using your fingertip, lightly brush the edges with water. Fold the skins over the filling into triangles and use a fork to gently crimp the edges closed.

LINE a plate with paper towels and set aside. Heat 2 inches oil in a deep heavy-bottomed skillet over high heat until very hot. (Dip a corner of a pot sticker in the oil and if it sizzles, it's ready.) Working in batches so as not to overcrowd the pan, fry the pot stickers until crispy and golden brown, about 2 minutes per side. Remove the pot stickers to the lined plate.

WHISK together the soy sauce, vinegar, and crushed red pepper in a small bowl. Serve immediately with the sauce on the side.

Sweet and Salty Mixed Nuts

JAKE: Tamari almonds are such a great snack, and if you make a big batch ahead of time, you can always have something gourmet ready for those grab-and-run days. They're also a fun little side snack near the cheese plate at your next gathering.

MAKES 2½ CUPS

1½ cups raw unsalted almonds
1 cup salted macadamia nuts
½ cup tamari

2 tablespoons sugar
Nonstick cooking spray

PREHEAT the oven to 400°F.

SPREAD almonds and macadamia nuts in an even layer on a rimmed baking sheet. Roast the nuts until fragrant and golden, about 8 minutes.

WHISK together the tamari and sugar in a medium bowl. While the nuts are still hot, transfer to the bowl and toss with the tamari until evenly coated.

SPRAY the baking sheet with cooking spray. Using a slotted spoon to let the liquid drip back into the bowl, spread the nuts on the baking sheet. Roast until the nuts look shiny and the glaze has set, about 8 minutes.

IMMEDIATELY remove the nuts to a plate and spread out to cool slightly. Once completely cool, store the nuts in an airtight container at room temperature for up to 1 week.

Honey-Crunch Granola

JURNEE: I am always on the go. Often my mornings are spent rushing out of the house to get to an appointment. Being a new mom, I found it somewhat difficult to tackle the morning time crunch and still have time to eat. My solution was this honey-crunch granola. Not only is it delicious, but it's super easy to make and most of the ingredients can be found already in your pantry. You have some oats, almonds, and honey in the house? *Voilà!* It also can be made in bulk and stored for later. I like to throw it on Greek yogurt or just keep a bag of it in my purse to snack on throughout the day. MAKES ABOUT 3 CUPS

---

2 cups quick-cooking oats
¼ cup finely diced dried apricots
¼ cup pumpkin seeds
¼ cup finely diced pitted dates
2 teaspoons ground cinnamon
¼ teaspoon sea salt

1½ teaspoons unrefined coconut oil, melted
½ cup unsweetened flaked coconut
2 teaspoons pure vanilla extract
½ cup honey
1 egg white, lightly whisked with a fork

PREHEAT the oven to 350°F.

MIX together all the ingredients in a large bowl.

TRANSFER the mixture to a large rimmed baking sheet and bake until the granola is golden brown, crispy, and starting to clump together, 10 to 12 minutes. Give the mixture a stir a couple of times while baking to be sure nothing sticks to the baking sheet. Set aside to cool. Store in an airtight container at room temperature for up to 2 weeks.

Homemade Potato Chips and Caramelized Onion Dip

JURNEE: I love to play around in the kitchen and make items found in an ordinary grocery store. After all, when food is made at home, you know more about the quality of the ingredients. Young (and not so young) members of the family get a kick out of eating warm, freshly made chips. Here's a simple and fun recipe, made only with ingredients you can pronounce!

MAKES A BIG BOWL OF CHIPS AND 3 CUPS DIP, TO SERVE 4 TO 6

CARAMELIZED ONION DIP
4 tablespoons (½ stick) salted butter
2 yellow onions, halved and thinly sliced
1 teaspoon Worcestershire sauce
½ teaspoon sea salt, plus more to taste
1 teaspoon granulated garlic
1 teaspoon granulated onion

1 cup sour cream
1 cup nonfat Greek yogurt

POTATO CHIPS
3 russet potatoes, scrubbed
Vegetable oil, for frying
Sea salt

MELT the butter in a large cast-iron skillet over high heat. Add the onions, reduce the heat to medium-low, and sweat until the onions have completely softened and browned, about 30 minutes. Keep an eye on the onions and stir often to be sure they don't burn. Add the Worcestershire, salt, granulated garlic, and granulated onion and cook 5 minutes, stirring occasionally. Remove from the heat and set aside to cool slightly. Transfer the onions to a cutting board and chop them finely.

COMBINE the sour cream, yogurt, and onions in a medium bowl. Stir to combine, and season with additional salt to taste, and stir again. Cover and refrigerate until ready to serve. This can be made up to 3 days in advance.

CUT the potatoes into ⅛-inch slices, setting them in a large bowl of cold water as you finish. Let the potatoes soak for 5 minutes, then drain them and spread them on paper towels to dry completely.

HEAT ½ inch oil in a large cast-iron skillet or heavy-bottomed frying pan over high heat until very hot. (Dip one end of a potato slice in the oil and if it sizzles, the oil is ready.) Working in batches so as not to overcrowd the skillet, fry the chips until brown and crispy, about 8 minutes. Remove to paper towels and season generously with salt. Serve immediately.

Matzo Bark

JAZZ: When most of us were kids, Blockbuster still existed. For those of you too young to remember, this was a store where you could go and pick out movies on video to rent. On movie nights, we usually ordered pizza or made something quick like tacos, but we always made snacks to eat while watching our video rentals. This was one of the favorites. These little delights are so easy to make, and they're the perfect snack for movie nights. Serve them in a decorative dish for a party!   MAKES 6 TO 8 SERVINGS

Baking spray
6 matzo sheets
2 cups sugar
½ cup heavy cream

3 tablespoons salted butter
½ teaspoon sea salt
1 cup bittersweet chocolate chips
¼ cup unsweetened flaked coconut

SPECIAL EQUIPMENT: candy thermometer

ARRANGE your fridge to accommodate two rimmed baking sheets. Line the baking sheets with foil and lightly spray the foil with baking spray. Lay 3 matzo sheets on each baking sheet.

COMBINE the sugar and ¼ cup water in a medium saucepan fitted with a candy thermometer. Cook the mixture over medium heat until it reaches 270°F and turns a deep amber color. Remove the caramel from the heat and add the heavy cream and butter. The mixture will bubble up but stir with a heat-proof rubber spatula or a wooden spoon until it's smooth. Let the caramel cool a couple of minutes, then very carefully ladle it over the matzo, using the bottom of the ladle to spread the caramel evenly. Use up all the caramel mixture before it sets too much in the pan. Evenly sprinkle the salt over the caramel.

PLACE the chocolate in a small microwave-safe bowl and heat on high for 1 minute. Remove and stir until completely smooth. Using a spoon, drizzle the melted chocolate over the matzo sheets in a decorative pattern. Immediately sprinkle with the coconut flakes, then place in the fridge to set the chocolate, about 10 minutes. Remove the bark to a cutting board and cut it into pieces; each can have a different shape and size. Serve immediately or store in an airtight container at room temperature for up to 1 week.

Pralines

JURNEE: I tend to like any combination of nuts and caramel flavor, so pralines are right up my alley. Whenever I'm working in the South, which is very often, I find a local praline shop. It's a treat that's hard to find anywhere else, so at home, I love making my own! They're delicious and they make the perfect gift.

MAKES 24 PRALINES

1 cup light brown sugar
1 cup granulated sugar
4 tablespoons (½ stick) salted butter
¼ cup plus 2 tablespoons whole milk

1 teaspoon pure vanilla extract
2 cups pecans, roughly chopped into
   large pieces

SPECIAL EQUIPMENT: candy thermometer

LINE a baking sheet with foil.

COMBINE the sugars, butter, ¼ cup of the milk, and the vanilla in a medium saucepan fitted with a candy thermometer. Bring the mixture to a boil, then reduce the heat and simmer until the sugar reaches 240°F, about 13 minutes. Stir in the pecans, making sure they are completely coated with sugar. Remove from the heat and stir in the remaining 2 tablespoons milk.

CAREFULLY scoop 1 tablespoon of the mixture onto the prepared baking sheet and spread it to form a small round praline. Working quickly while the sugar is still liquid, repeat to make the rest of the pralines, leaving about 1 inch between each one. Let the pralines cool for 15 minutes to set.

SERVE immediately or store in an airtight container at room temperature for up to 2 weeks.

Warm Toffee Peanuts

JAZZ: Snowy days were the most exciting part of living in New York as a kid. Snow also meant the holidays, and nothing reminds me of holiday time in New York more than the smell of toffee nuts and steam coming from the carts that sell them. These peanuts are a take on those delicious toffee nuts.

You could substitute any nut for the peanuts in this recipe—it would be delicious with almonds, cashews, or even pecans.

MAKES 10 TO 12 SERVINGS

Nonstick cooking spray
1 pound unsalted dry-roasted peanuts
    (about 3 cups)
1 teaspoon ground cinnamon
1 teaspoon sea salt

2 cups sugar
4 tablespoons (½ stick) salted butter
¼ cup light corn syrup
1 teaspoon pure vanilla extract

SPECIAL EQUIPMENT: candy thermometer

LINE a rimmed baking sheet with foil and lightly spray it with cooking spray.

PLACE the nuts in a large bowl and spray them lightly with cooking spray. Sprinkle the cinnamon and salt over the nuts and toss to coat them evenly. Set aside.

COMBINE the sugar, butter, corn syrup, vanilla, and 2 tablespoons water in a medium saucepan fitted with a candy thermometer. Cook the mixture over medium heat, stirring only once or twice, until it reaches the soft-crack stage, 280°F.

IMMEDIATELY pour the nuts into the hot sugar mixture, stirring as you go so they're evenly coated with the sugar, and then quickly and carefully pour the nuts onto the prepared baking sheet. Spread them out and let them cool for 15 minutes.

BREAK the nuts into small clusters and serve immediately, or store in an airtight container at room temperature for up to 3 weeks.

Ginger-Spiced Applesauce

JAZZ: I want my daughter, Nylah, to enjoy her food as much as I do, and I began experimenting with applesauce after she started eating solid food. I didn't want her to have just any basic applesauce, so I mixed a variety of apples and created the perfect balance of sweet and sour and added a little warmth with some ginger. She has always loved this recipe—she's been eating it for three years now. Motherhood achievements!

MAKES 2 CUPS

2 Gala apples, peeled, cored, and cut into ½-inch dice

2 Granny Smith apples, peeled, cored, and cut into ½-inch dice

⅓ cup unsweetened apple juice

2-inch fresh ginger knob, peeled and halved

PLACE all the ingredients in a medium skillet or saucepan with a lid and bring to a boil. Reduce the heat to low, cover, and simmer until the apples are knife tender and soft, about 12 minutes.

CAREFULLY remove the ginger and discard. Transfer the apple mixture to a blender and blend until completely smooth, about 1 minute.

LET cool and serve immediately. Store the applesauce in an airtight container in the fridge for up to 1 week.

SATURDAY
Brunch

JAZZ: Whenever we moved across the country, we'd drive straight through in three days. Hotel stays were a rare luxury; we'd nap in the car and wake to find we'd almost made it through another state. We'd closely watch the mile markers on the side of the road as they counted up or down, depending on the direction we were headed. We crossed the lowlands of Pennsylvania, the farmlands of Indiana, the Rocky Mountains of Utah, seeing cows, goats, horses, and barnyards along the way. We'd wave at truck drivers and signal them to blow their loud horns for us as we passed.

Food stops were a time to stretch our legs and get a glimpse of the food culture of the town we were in. We'd spend mornings in diners enjoying one another's company over long breakfast breaks before hitting the road again. We'd often travel during winter, with icy roads and freezing temperatures, so diners were a nice, warm respite to sit and enjoy sweet pancakes, salty meats, and a warm cup of hot chocolate. When we started taking the southern route through Arizona, Texas, and Alabama, we experienced a whole other food culture.

At home, we turned our love of breakfast into a brunch ritual. Brunch meant staying in pajamas, eating all day, and watching movies until dark. There's something so very comforting about noshing on brunch foods all day long. Our love of these sweet and savory days continues even now. Hope you find these recipes as sweet and wonderful as we do. Here's to warm gatherings around the brunch table!

Shrimp and Grits

Any dish that has shrimp, grits, and bacon in it, sign me up!

MAKES 4 MAIN OR 6 APPETIZER SERVINGS

GRITS

1 teaspoon sea salt

¾ cup quick-cooking hominy grits

1 tablespoon salted butter

SHRIMP

4 slices thick-cut bacon, sliced

6 garlic cloves, minced

¼ cup minced yellow onion

¼ cup finely diced red bell pepper

¼ cup finely diced green bell pepper

¼ cup fresh oregano leaves, minced

1 pound medium shrimp, peeled, deveined, and tails removed

½ teaspoon sea salt

½ teaspoon paprika

1 teaspoon gumbo filé

¼ teaspoon cayenne pepper

2 tablespoons unbleached all-purpose flour

1½ cups low-sodium chicken stock

TO make the grits, bring 3 cups water to a boil in a medium saucepan. Add the salt, then slowly whisk in the grits and cook until they are smooth, with no clumps, about 1 minute. Reduce the heat to low, cover, and cook 5 to 6 minutes, stirring occasionally, until thickened and pulling away from sides of pot. Remove from the heat and stir in the butter. Cover and set aside until the shrimp is ready.

LINE a plate with paper towels and set aside. To make the shrimp sauce, arrange the bacon in a large cast-iron skillet or heavy-bottomed frying pan over high heat and cook until crispy, 3 to 4 minutes on each side. Remove the bacon to the lined plate to absorb the excess oil. Reserve 2 tablespoons of the bacon grease in the skillet. When the bacon is cool enough to handle, chop it roughly and set aside.

PLACE the skillet over low heat. Add the garlic, onion, bell peppers, and 2 tablespoons of the oregano to the pan and sauté until softened, about 6 minutes. Increase the heat to medium, add the shrimp, and season with the salt, paprika, gumbo filé, and cayenne. Sprinkle the flour on top and toss the shrimp to coat them evenly. Cook until the shrimp is opaque and pink, about 5 minutes.

GENTLY stir in the stock. Reduce the heat and simmer until the sauce has thickened and turned a dark brown hue, about 8 minutes.

PLATE the grits, lay a few shrimp on top, and sprinkle on some crunchy bacon bits and a little of the remaining oregano. *Voilà!*

Country Breakfast

JURNEE: When we were kids, many Saturday mornings consisted of the Looney Tunes on TV, Anita Baker blasting, and a big country breakfast. With six kids, big dishes were always on the menu, but who says big has to be boring? Our version of country breakfast brings you a few breakfast favorites together in one unique dish.

MAKES 6 SERVINGS

---

5 slices thick-cut applewood-smoked bacon

4 garlic cloves, minced

½ cup finely diced yellow onion

¼ yellow bell pepper, cored, seeded, and finely diced

¼ red bell pepper, cored, seeded, and finely diced

6 ounces smoked beef sausage, quartered and sliced

8 baby red potatoes, scrubbed and cut into small dice (about 2 cups)

2 teaspoons dried basil

¼ teaspoon crushed red pepper

1 teaspoon paprika

¼ teaspoon sea salt

3 cremini mushrooms, finely diced (about ½ cup)

1 cup chopped baby spinach

5 eggs, lightly whisked with a fork

1 cup grated white Cheddar (about 4 ounces)

Handful of fresh basil leaves, chopped

PREHEAT the oven to 375°F.

LINE a plate with paper towels and set aside. Arrange the bacon in a medium cast-iron skillet or an ovenproof pan over high heat and cook until crispy, 3 to 4 minutes on each side. Remove to the lined plate to absorb the excess oil. Reserve 2 tablespoons of the bacon grease in the skillet. When the bacon is cool enough to handle, chop it roughly and set aside.

PLACE the skillet over medium heat. Add the garlic, onion, bell peppers, and sausage, give the mixture a stir, and spread it evenly in the skillet. Cook until the sausage is brown and crispy, 5 minutes, stirring occasionally.

Add the potatoes, basil, crushed red pepper, paprika, and salt and stir to combine. Reduce the heat to medium, cover, and cook until the potatoes are tender, about 12 minutes, stirring halfway through to be sure nothing is burning on the bottom. Add the mushrooms, bacon, and spinach; give it a stir; and cook 2 minutes, until the spinach is wilted.

POUR the eggs over the mixture and spread them out to be sure they're evenly distributed. Sprinkle with the cheese and bake until the eggs are set and the cheese is melted, 10 to 12 minutes. Cut into wedges, garnish with the basil, and serve.

Croissant French Toast

JUSSIE: Years ago, I went to Zurich for work and stumbled on this tiny Haitian spot. Their food is brought in fresh every day and once they run out for the day, they close. I was expecting Haitian food, and that's what I wanted. Then I saw French toast on the menu. Haitian French toast? That made complete and absolute sense to me. The owner, Soney—a small sweet woman who smelled like daisies—said they had run out of the special bread for the French toast and asked if she should just use another bread. Listen, I'm not saditty, and I don't want to be the typical annoying, demanding American, so I went along with it. When she brought out French toast made with *croissants*, I knew that Soney's little Haitian restaurant in Zurich had changed my life forever.

MAKES 4 TO 6 SERVINGS

MAPLE-ALMOND SYRUP

½ cup chopped unsalted raw almonds
¼ cup raisins
1 cup pure maple syrup

WHIPPED CREAM

½ cup heavy cream
¼ cup confectioners' sugar

TOAST

2 eggs
3 tablespoons pure maple syrup
1 tablespoon ground cinnamon
¼ teaspoon ground nutmeg
Pinch of salt
3 tablespoons salted butter
6 croissants, split as for a sandwich

TO make the syrup, toast the almonds in a medium saucepan over low heat until golden brown, about 2 minutes. Stir often and be careful not to let them burn. Add the raisins and maple syrup, stir, and cook for 2 minutes, until the syrup is warmed through and the raisins have softened a bit. Turn off the burner and cover the pan to keep warm.

USING a hand beater or whisk, in a medium bowl whip together the cream and sugar until peaks hold. Refrigerate until ready to serve.

WHISK together the eggs, maple syrup, cinnamon, nutmeg, and salt in a baking dish (at least 8 × 8 inches). Melt 1 tablespoon of the butter in a large cast-iron skillet over high heat. While the butter is melting, dip 4 croissant slices in the egg batter, letting any excess drip off. Transfer the slices to the skillet and cook until browned and slightly crisp, about 2 minutes, then flip and cook the other side for 1 minute more. Be sure to press the slices down with a spatula to help them get nice and crispy. Remove the toast to a platter while you make the other two batches.

SERVE the French toast with a big drizzle of maple-almond syrup and a spoonful of whipped cream.

Shrimp Omelet

JURNEE: It's almost as if Mommy was mother to our entire neighborhood—Mother to the World! She's always loved feeding our friends; they became so accustomed to her putting food in their bellies that they'd come over and sweet-talk her into making their favorite dish. She often served breakfast for dinner, and one of the most popular items on the menu was her shrimp omelet. No one could make an omelet like Mommy. These go well with the Mini Butter Biscuits (page 208). **MAKES 1 SERVING**

---

3 eggs, beaten
1 slice bacon, cooked and chopped
½ Roma tomato, seeded and diced
1 tablespoon thinly sliced green onion
2 teaspoons chopped fresh basil
Freshly ground black pepper

1 tablespoon salted butter
3 medium shrimp, peeled, deveined, and
    tails removed, cut into ½-inch dice
1 garlic clove, minced
¼ cup shredded Monterey Jack

WHISK together the eggs, bacon, tomato, green onion, basil, and a grind or two of pepper. Set aside.

MELT ½ tablespoon of the butter in an 8-inch nonstick pan over medium heat. Add the shrimp and garlic and sauté until the shrimp is almost pink, about 1 minute.

ADD the remaining ½ tablespoon butter. Pour in the egg mixture and cook until it starts to set along the edges, about 1 minute. Tilt the pan and lift the edges of the omelet so that any uncooked egg runs underneath the cooked parts. Using a spatula, fold the egg in half and flip. Sprinkle with cheese and let cook an additional minute, until the cheese is melted. Serve immediately.

Strawberry-Cream Cheese Waffles

JURNEE: On a trip to Belgium, I remember being blown away by the abundant waffle shops everywhere. The scent of freshly made waffles would fill the streets, and it seemed as if every block I walked down had a different waffle shop tempting me with that sweet aroma.

This recipe turns the traditional Belgian waffle on its head. Cream cheese "whipped cream" and minty strawberries inside a succulent waffle make for an all-around heavenly time. MAKES 12 SERVINGS

STRAWBERRIES
1 pint fresh strawberries, hulled and cut into small dice
2 tablespoons granulated sugar
½ tablespoon finely chopped fresh mint

WAFFLES
2 cups unbleached all-purpose flour
4 teaspoons baking powder
4 tablespoons (½ stick) salted butter, melted
1 teaspoon pure vanilla extract
½ teaspoon ground cinnamon
1½ cups whole milk
¼ cup agave
2 eggs

12 mint leaves

CREAM CHEESE TOPPING
8 ounces cream cheese, at room temperature
½ cup confectioners' sugar
1 teaspoon pure vanilla extract

COMBINE the strawberries, sugar, and chopped mint in a medium bowl. Let the berries macerate for 30 minutes, until they have softened and the juices release.

MEANWHILE, make the waffle batter. Whisk together the flour, baking powder, butter, vanilla, cinnamon, milk, agave, and eggs in a large bowl.

PREHEAT a waffle maker and cook the waffles until golden and set. (My 6-inch waffle maker makes 6 waffles from this batter.) Cut the waffles into quarters.

WHISK together in a medium bowl the cream cheese, sugar, and vanilla until smooth.

TO assemble, place one waffle quarter on a plate and top with 2 tablespoons of the cream cheese topping. Place another waffle quarter on top and add 1 tablespoon topping, ¼ cup of the strawberries, and a mint leaf for garnish.

Buckwheat Banana Pancakes

JURNEE: Songs have been written about legendary banana pancakes, which have brought sunshine to many early mornings but are equally savored as breakfast for dinner. With this simple batter, you'll be enjoying these favorites in under thirty minutes. Feel free to sop up all the maple syrup or honey you can with each bite. Long live banana pancakes!

MAKES TWELVE TO FOURTEEN 6-INCH PANCAKES

---

2 cups buckwheat flour

2 teaspoons ground cinnamon

½ teaspoon ground nutmeg

½ teaspoon sea salt

1 teaspoon baking powder

1 teaspoon pure vanilla extract

¼ cup unrefined coconut oil, melted

1½ cups whole milk

¼ cup honey

2 eggs, whisked

1½ ripe bananas, sliced into ¼-inch rounds

Salted butter, for frying

Maple syrup or honey, for serving

WHISK together the flour, cinnamon, nutmeg, salt, and baking powder in a large bowl. Add the vanilla, oil, milk, honey, and eggs and whisk until just smooth (do not overmix). Gently fold in the banana slices.

MELT ½ tablespoon butter in a large cast-iron skillet or nonstick griddle pan over medium-high heat. Working in batches so as not to overcrowd the skillet, measure ¼ cup batter for each pancake and pour into the hot skillet. Cook for about 3 minutes, until small bubbles appear along the edges, then flip and cook for about 2 minutes, until browned. Place the cooked pancakes in the oven on a low temperature of 150°F to keep them warm. Repeat to make the rest of the pancakes, adding another ½ tablespoon butter per batch.

SERVE with maple syrup or honey.

Mini Butter Biscuits

JURNEE: Brunch would not be complete without these traditional little biscuits. They're so fluffy, a perfect complement to your favorite topping, whether butter, strawberry jam, or honey. Happy brunching! Try these with Country Breakfast (page 199) or Shrimp Omelet (page 203).

MAKES 25 TO 30 BISCUITS

2 cups unbleached all-purpose flour, plus more for rolling out the dough

5 teaspoons baking powder

¼ teaspoon sea salt

4 tablespoons (½ stick) cold salted butter, cut into cubes

4 tablespoons unrefined coconut oil, melted

1½ cups buttermilk

Salted butter, softened, for serving (optional)

Honey or jam, for serving (optional)

PREHEAT the oven to 350°F. Line two rimmed baking sheets with parchment paper and set aside.

WHISK together the flour, baking powder, and salt in a large bowl. Use your hands to work the butter and 2 tablespoons of the oil into the dry mixture until it looks like it has pebbles in it. Pour in the buttermilk and gently bring the dough together, taking care not to overwork it.

LIGHTLY dust a clean work surface and your hands with flour and turn out the dough. Use your hands to bring the dough together and flatten it to ½ inch thick. Use a mini biscuit cutter or champagne flute to cut rounds from the dough, dusting the cutter or flute so that the biscuits release easily. When you've cut all the rounds you can, bring the dough back together, flatten again, and cut more rounds until all the dough is used.

TRANSFER the rounds to the prepared baking sheets, setting them 2 inches apart. Brush the tops with the remaining 2 tablespoons oil. Bake until slightly golden and set, about 20 minutes.

SERVE with butter and honey or jam, if desired. These are best eaten the same day but you can rewarm them to eat the next day.

Home Fries

JAKE: Home fries are the kind of down-home dish that we just can't live without; there's nothing like a good side of home-fried potatoes to round out your brunch plate. These are particularly good because we use roasted red potatoes. Tossed with olive oil and spices, they're simple yet perfect.

MAKES 4 TO 6 SERVINGS

4 large red potatoes, cut into ½-inch dice (about 5 cups)
¼ cup plus 2 tablespoons olive oil
½ teaspoon sea salt

1 tablespoon granulated onion
2 teaspoons granulated garlic
1 tablespoon dried dill

PREHEAT the oven to 400°F.

SPREAD the potatoes on a large rimmed baking sheet and toss with the rest of the ingredients.

BAKE until golden brown and knife tender, about 45 minutes. Make sure to take the potatoes out every 10 minutes or so and toss them around to be sure they don't stick to the baking sheet and all sides get golden. Enjoy!

Cinnamon-Raisin Sweet Rolls

JAZZ: When we were young, we lived in Cincinnati, Ohio, for a few months as we made our way back to California from New York. We made friends with a family that lived on the outskirts of the city, in a rural area. The family had three kids and at the time we had five, and we all became very close. They lived on eleven majestic acres of land, but best of all they had a swimming pool, which was incredible to us city kids. It was the coldest pool ever, and I think Jojo had to save Jussie from drowning on one occasion, but other than that it was a cool pool. The best part about sleepovers at their house was waking up to the smell of cinnamon rolls baking in the oven. I've never forgotten the magic of these cinnamon rolls, and just for fun I decided to create a recipe myself, so in a few years when my daughter has sleepovers I can impress her friends with my fragrant cinnamon-raisin sweet rolls. Enjoy sweet cinnamon roll kisses!

MAKES 16 MEDIUM SWEET ROLLS

SWEET ROLLS

1 cup whole milk

Two ¼-ounce packs active dry yeast (about 4½ teaspoons)

12 tablespoons (1½ sticks) unsalted butter

1 cup granulated sugar

2 large eggs

1 teaspoon pure vanilla extract

5½ cups unbleached all-purpose flour, plus more for rolling out the dough

2 tablespoons ground cinnamon

2 teaspoons kosher salt

1 teaspoon vegetable oil

1½ cups packed light brown sugar

2 cups raisins

GLAZE

2 cups confectioners' sugar

¼ cup whole milk

2 teaspoons pure vanilla extract

PREHEAT the oven to 350°F.

HEAT the milk in a medium saucepan over medium-high heat until it is just warm to the touch (110°F to 115°F). Pour the milk into a small bowl and stir in the yeast. Let the mixture stand for 5 minutes, until the yeast becomes foamy.

MELT 8 tablespoons (1 stick) of the butter in the same saucepan. Whisk in the sugar, eggs, and vanilla until the mixture is smooth. When the yeast is foamy, whisk in the milk mixture.

WHISK together the flour, 1 tablespoon of the cinnamon, and the salt in a medium bowl. Make a well in the center of the flour and pour in half of the liquid mixture. Fold the ingredients together with a rubber spatula. Add in the remaining half of the liquid and fold the dough together until it forms a ball and you no longer see any flour. Lightly dust a clean work surface and your hands with

flour, turn out the dough, and knead until smooth.

CLEAN out the medium bowl and lightly grease it with the oil. Place the dough in the greased bowl, cover, and set in a warm place to rise for 1 hour.

LIGHTLY flour a clean work surface and your hands, then turn out the dough and roll into an 18 × 24-inch rectangle. Melt the remaining 4 tablespoons (½ stick) butter and brush the dough with the butter. Mix together the brown sugar and the remaining 1 tablespoon cinnamon and sprinkle the dough with the mixture, lightly pressing the sugar into the butter so it sticks. Evenly spread the raisins over the cinnamon sugar. Working on the long side, roll the dough into a tight log. If the log gets longer than

24 inches, lift up the ends and press the dough toward the center, then trim the ends of the log so it is exactly 24 inches long.

CUT the log into sixteen 1½-inch rolls and set them in a 9 × 13-inch baking dish or two 9-inch cast-iron skillets. Bake for 25 to 30 minutes, or until the sugar bubbles around the edges, the cinnamon rolls are golden brown, and the tops feel firm when lightly pressed with a rubber spatula. Let cool for 15 minutes.

MEANWHILE, to make the glaze, whisk together the confectioners' sugar, milk, and vanilla in a medium bowl. Pour the glaze over the warm sweet rolls and serve immediately or keep covered at room temperature for up to 2 days.

Jewish Deli Deviled Eggs

JAKE: All things I typically love on a bagel are put into these deviled eggs. With chunky smoked salmon, red onion, and cream cheese in every bite, they are devilishly delicious.   MAKES 24 DEVILED EGGS

1 dozen eggs
One 4-ounce package sliced smoked
   salmon
½ cup mayonnaise
½ teaspoon paprika

¼ teaspoon cayenne pepper
½ teaspoon kosher salt
Minced fresh chives
¼ red onion, finely diced

PLACE the eggs in large saucepan, add cold water to cover, and bring to a boil. Turn off the heat and let the eggs sit for exactly 12 minutes. Meanwhile, prepare an ice water bath. When the eggs are done, transfer them to the bath and let them sit for 5 minutes, until completely cool. Peel the eggs, cut them in half lengthwise, and gently remove the yolks to a medium bowl. Set the whites on a rimmed platter.

SET two slices of smoked salmon to the side. Chop the remaining slices finely and place them in the bowl with the egg yolks. Add the mayonnaise, paprika, cayenne, and salt and mash gently with a fork until the mixture is smooth and incorporated.

CUT the reserved salmon into 1-inch slices. Fill each of the egg whites with a heaping teaspoon of the egg yolk mixture, then garnish with the sliced salmon, chives, and onion.

Peach-Applesauce Muffins

JAZZ: These beautiful muffins are an awesome addition to any brunch menu. The applesauce makes them super moist, and they are just as delicious the following day as a snack or with breakfast. These muffins are so light and delicious!

MAKES 15 MUFFINS

1 cup whole wheat flour
½ cup wheat germ
2 teaspoons baking soda
½ teaspoon sea salt
½ cup unsweetened flaked coconut
2 teaspoons ground cinnamon
2 eggs
1 teaspoon pure vanilla extract
½ cup honey

¾ cup canned peaches in unsweetened juice, drained and mashed
½ cup unsweetened applesauce
¼ cup grapeseed oil
¼ cup finely grated carrots
½ cup raisins

SPECIAL EQUIPMENT: two muffin tins, muffin liners

PREHEAT the oven to 350°F. Line one standard muffin tin plus three of the cups in a second muffin tin with liners or grease each cup.

WHISK together the flour, wheat germ, baking soda, salt, coconut, and cinnamon in a large bowl. Whisk together in a medium bowl the eggs, vanilla, honey, peaches, applesauce, and oil until fully incorporated.

Add the wet mixture to the dry mixture and mix until just incorporated (do not overmix). Fold in the carrots and raisins.

USING a ¼ cup measure, scoop batter into each liner. Bake for 20 minutes, until a toothpick comes out clean. Let the muffins cool for at least 15 minutes before serving. Store leftover muffins in a zip-top bag in the fridge for up to 4 days.

FOUR MUST-HAVE ARTISAN BUTTERS

JAKE: Butter rules the world, or at least it should rule the world. I've bowed down to butter ever since I was a two-year-old getting caught in the fridge eating butter right out of the container. Making flavored butters is fun and easy to do; check out these four (three savory, one sweet) and turn them into an epic butter spread served with various sweet and savory breads, crackers, and muffins for family and friends, or have a pretty great party by yourself.

Apple Butter

This sweet butter is great on biscuits, corn bread, pancakes, and muffins.   MAKES ABOUT 1½ CUPS BUTTER

1 Honeycrisp apple, peeled, cored, and
   cut into ½-inch dice
¼ cup pure apple juice
½ teaspoon ground cinnamon

2 pinches of sea salt
1 tablespoon brown sugar
8 tablespoons (1 stick) unsalted butter,
   at room temperature

COMBINE the apple, juice, cinnamon, salt, and brown sugar in a small saucepan and cook over medium heat until the apple softens, 7 minutes. Let cool slightly.

TRANSFER the apple mixture to a food processor, add the butter, and puree until smooth.

STORE the butter in an airtight container in the fridge for up to 2 weeks.

Butters

chili

sundried
tomato
shallot

apple

rosemary
garlic

Rosemary-Garlic Butter

This savory butter is delicious on corn bread or in a simple yummy pasta. Try with Homemade Linguine (page 42)! MAKES ABOUT 1 CUP BUTTER

8 tablespoons (1 stick) unsalted butter, at room temperature
2 teaspoons finely chopped fresh rosemary

4 garlic cloves, finely minced
½ teaspoon sea salt

MIX all the ingredients in a medium bowl until they are fully incorporated.

STORE the butter in an airtight container in the fridge for up to 2 weeks.

Chili Butter

This butter is wonderful for the Charbroiled Oysters (page 89) but also works well on garlic bread or in place of the traditional butter in our Roasted Garlic Mashed Potatoes (page 131). MAKES 1 CUP BUTTER

½ pound (2 sticks) salted butter
16 garlic cloves

2 teaspoons dried oregano
½ teaspoon crushed red pepper

PUREE the butter, garlic, oregano, and red pepper flakes in a food processor until completely smooth.

STORE the butter in an airtight container in the fridge for up to 2 weeks.

Sun-Dried Tomato-Shallot Butter

Try this butter on sourdough bread alongside Spaghetti and Chicken Meatballs (page 62).

MAKES ABOUT 1½ CUPS BUTTER

---

1 cup sundried tomatoes packed in oil, drained and finely diced

1 medium shallot, finely diced

¼ teaspoon sea salt

8 tablespoons (1 stick) unsalted butter, at room temperature

COOK the tomatoes and shallot in a small saucepan over medium heat until the shallot softens, about 2 minutes. Set aside to cool slightly.

USING a rubber spatula, in a medium bowl mix together the tomato-shallot mixture, salt, and butter until smooth.

STORE the butter in an airtight container in the fridge for up to 2 weeks.

MORE SWEETS, *Please*

JAZZ: A new life is a joy to be celebrated, especially when Mom's cravings mean the whole family gets to eat home-baked desserts! Whenever she was pregnant or breastfeeding, which was pretty much the entire time we were growing up, our mom had the desire to bake. Her specialties were oatmeal-raisin cookies, homemade ice cream, and various pies.

It was probably part of the nesting, but everything had to be made from scratch, just the way her own mother baked. Our grandmother was a single mom and a domestic worker who spent much of her time taking care of other people's homes, but on weekends and for birthdays, she enjoyed making a host of tantalizing desserts.

Life is somehow a lot faster nowadays than it was in our grandmother's or mom's times, but it's still fun and delicious to spend slow weekends creating wonderful desserts. I inherited the joy of making desserts and love the creativity involved in the whole process. From the moment of conception, the dessert starts as an idea and is transformed through an intricate process of measuring, whipping, and tasting until the moment of euphoria is reached and the divine dessert is revealed. Baking brings out your inner *artiste*, and your imagination can run wild. Whether you're following a recipe or creating your own, baking is an art of creation that you can take pride in. You know you'll come out with something both delicious and beautiful.

Citrus Sorbet with Limoncello

JURNEE: This is a very grown-up version of a childhood favorite, lemon Italian ice. It's the perfect way to cool off on a hot summer day or cozy up with any time of year. To make it kid friendly, just skip the limoncello!

MAKES 4 TO 6 SERVINGS

---

1 cup sugar
½ cup loosely packed fresh mint
1 tablespoon lemon zest
1½ cups fresh lemon juice (about 6 large lemons)
1 tablespoon orange zest

Juice of 1 orange (about ¼ cup)
Zest of 1 lime
Limoncello, for serving
Small mint sprigs

SPECIAL EQUIPMENT: ice cream maker

PLACE the bowl of an ice cream maker in the freezer.

BRING to a boil the sugar and 1 cup water in a small saucepan. Cook, stirring, until the sugar is dissolved, about 10 minutes. Remove from the heat, add the mint, and steep until cooled, about 15 minutes. Strain the mint simple syrup into a medium bowl and add the fruit zests and juices and ½ cup water. Stir to combine.

REMOVE the frozen bowl from the freezer, pour in the mixture, and churn according to the manufacturer's instructions. Transfer the sorbet to a deep 8 × 8-inch baking dish or standard loaf pan, cover tightly with plastic wrap, and freeze for at least 4 hours or up to overnight.

TO serve, scoop the sorbet into a small serving bowl, drizzle with limoncello, and garnish with a sprig of mint.

Drunken Grilled Peaches with Vanilla and Lemon Mascarpone

JAZZ: I created this recipe one summer while visiting my aunt and uncle, who at the time were living in Atlanta. They love to entertain, and it was the Fourth of July, so of course there was a BBQ happening, with a green egg smoker and all. I wanted to make a dessert that was sophisticated, went well with the grilling theme, and would blow everyone's minds. Since we were in Georgia, peaches were a natural choice of fruit to grill. I created a sweet rub for my fruit, with spices inspired by our family peach cobbler. I knew my uncle had some bourbon around and that would give it the southern sophistication I was looking for. I have to say I blew my own mind—it was a big hit! Jazz's Famous Drunken Grilled Peaches were born! The rest is history. MAKES 12 SERVINGS

---

6 fresh peaches, halved and pitted
1½ cups bourbon
⅓ cup fresh lemon juice (about
    2 lemons), plus the zest of 1 lemon,
    reserved
2 tablespoons pure vanilla extract
8 ounces mascarpone
¼ cup heavy cream

3 tablespoons confectioners' sugar,
    sifted
Seeds of 1 vanilla bean split lengthwise
    and scraped
½ cup packed dark brown sugar
1½ teaspoons ground cinnamon
1½ teaspoons ground nutmeg
Mint sprigs for garnish

ARRANGE the peaches cut side up in a 9 × 13-inch glass baking dish.

WHISK together the bourbon, lemon juice, and vanilla in a medium bowl. Pour the bourbon mixture over the peaches and baste each peach to coat it well. Cover with plastic wrap and macerate at room temperature for 30 minutes.

MEANWHILE, in a medium bowl mix together the mascarpone, cream, confectioners' sugar, vanilla bean seeds, and lemon zest until smooth. Cover with plastic wrap and refrigerate. Remove from the fridge 20 minutes before serving.

HEAT a grill or grill pan over high heat.

USING your hands, rub the cut side of each peach with 2 teaspoons of the brown sugar. Sprinkle each peach with a pinch of the cinnamon and nutmeg. Place the peaches cut side down on the hot grill and cook until they are seared with grill marks and the sugar is caramelized, 6 to 8 minutes. Gently turn the peach slices over and grill for 4 minutes more, until slightly charred. Remove from the grill.

TOP each peach with a spoonful of the vanilla-lemon mascarpone, garnish with mint, and serve.

Lemon-Lavender Cupcakes

JAZZ: It took me three times to pass my driving test as a teenager, and it took me three times to get these cupcakes right last year. The lesson is, third time's the charm! This recipe is such a sweet surprise. I wanted to create a dessert that would be super cute for my daughter's second birthday. I *love* cooking with floral accents like lavender! I knew I wanted to use a natural sweetener, like honey, and that I wanted a strong but balanced lemon-lavender flavor. These little cuties are yummy and adorable, and they taste like spring. They can be served at a kids' party, a picnic, or an adult soiree!

MAKES 18 CUPCAKES

LAVENDER SUGAR
⅓ heaping cup dried lavender
¾ cup coconut palm sugar

CUPCAKES
½ pound (2 sticks) unsalted butter, at room temperature
¾ cup honey
2 large eggs, at room temperature
½ teaspoon lemon oil
3 cups unbleached all-purpose flour
2 teaspoons baking soda
1 teaspoon sea salt
½ cup fresh lemon juice (from 2 large lemons)
1 cup whole milk

¼ cup grated lemon zest (from 5 or 6 lemons)

LEMON FROSTING
8 ounces white chocolate, chopped
1 pound whipped cream cheese, at room temperature
8 tablespoons (1 stick) unsalted butter, at room temperature
1 teaspoon lemon oil
¼ teaspoon sea salt

18 seasonal edible flowers

SPECIAL EQUIPMENT: two cupcake tins, cupcake liners, a pastry bag (or a resealable plastic bag) fitted with a large star tip

TO make the lavender sugar, blend the lavender in a food processor or blender on high speed until finely ground. Remove 1 tablespoon of the lavender and set aside. Add the sugar to the remaining lavender and blend to a very fine powder. Store in an airtight container until ready to use.

PREHEAT the oven to 350°F.

CREAM the butter, honey, and 6 tablespoons of the lavender sugar in a stand mixer fitted with the paddle attachment. Add the eggs and lemon oil and mix until smooth.

WHISK together the flour, baking soda, salt, and the reserved 1 tablespoon of ground lavender in a medium bowl. With the mixer on low speed, slowly incorporate half the flour mixture, then mix in the lemon juice. (The mixture may look curdled but it is not.) Mix in the remaining flour mixture, then the milk and lemon zest. Continue mixing until the batter is totally smooth.

DOUBLE-LINE eighteen wells total in two standard nonstick cupcake tins. Fill each liner with a heaping ¼ cup of the batter and bake until a toothpick inserted into the center of the cupcakes comes out clean, 16 to 18 minutes. Let the cupcakes cool in the pans until easy to handle. Place 6 tablespoons of the lavender sugar in a shallow dish. While still slightly warm, dip the tops of the cupcakes in the lavender sugar. Place the cupcakes on a rimmed baking sheet and set aside to cool completely.

TO make the lemon frosting, melt the white chocolate over a double boiler. Let it cool slightly, but don't let it set. Whip the cream cheese, butter, lemon oil, and salt in the bowl of a stand mixer fitted with the whip attachment. Slowly add the melted white chocolate and mix until smooth. Spoon the frosting into a pastry bag fitted with a large star tip and refrigerate until set.

PIPE the frosting onto the cupcakes and garnish with the edible flowers. You'll want to serve these pretty quickly after frosting and garnishing, so feel free to make the cake part beforehand.

Honey-Vanilla Ice Cream

JUSSIE: Mommy is a legend for her sweets; she used to make ice cream as if her first name were Häagen and last name were Dazs. I love this simple but creamy ice cream.   MAKES ABOUT 2 PINTS

---

2 cups whole milk
2 cups heavy cream
2 tablespoons pure vanilla extract
5 egg yolks
½ cup honey

½ cup sugar
Honeycomb, for serving (optional)

SPECIAL EQUIPMENT: candy thermometer, ice cream maker

PLACE the bowl of an ice cream maker in the freezer.

COMBINE the milk, cream, and vanilla in a medium saucepan over medium heat just until you see the first bubble (don't let it scorch).

WHILE the milk mixture heats up, in a medium bowl whisk together the yolks, honey, and sugar until the sugar dissolves and the yolks turn a light yellow color. When the milk is hot, drizzle about 1 cup into the egg yolks and immediately whisk to combine. This will temper the egg yolks and keep them from cooking. Reduce the heat to medium-low and pour the tempered eggs into the hot milk, stirring constantly, until the mixture reaches approximately 170°F on a candy thermometer and coats the back of a spoon. Immediately strain the custard into a large bowl and set it on the counter to cool completely.

REMOVE the bowl from the freezer.

FREEZE the custard in your ice cream maker according to the manufacturer's instructions, then transfer the ice cream to an airtight container and freeze until ready to serve.

SCOOP the ice cream into small serving bowls and, if desired, top with crumbled honeycomb.

Perfect Piecrust

When Mom gave me this recipe, she presented it like a secret omen, a rare piece of knowledge. She said, "When I used to make this, I'd say to myself, Let me pay attention to the exact process of what I'm doing, because one day I'll have to explain this recipe to someone, and it will probably be Jazz."

The secret to a perfect piecrust every time is that your butter is very cold and you use ice water. This will make your piecrust perfectly soft and flaky. As Mom says, "Nothing will make you madder than a tough piecrust!" (I took a couple of small liberties with this crust and added sugar and vanilla. Shhh, don't tell my mom!)

This crust works for any of the pie recipes in this chapter. For the Mini Vegan Sweet Potato Pies (page 233), substitute a vegan butter such as Earth Balance for the butter.

MAKES ENOUGH DOUGH FOR TWO 9-INCH SINGLE-CRUST PIES OR 1 DOUBLE-CRUST PIE

---

2 cups unbleached all-purpose flour, plus more for handling the dough
1 tablespoon sugar

½ pound (2 sticks) cold, salted butter, cut into ½-inch pieces
1 teaspoon pure vanilla extract
3 to 4 tablespoons ice-cold water

MIX together the flour and sugar in a large bowl. Add the butter and use your hands to press and pinch the flour mixture into the butter, working until the mixture resembles coarse cornmeal (see Cook's Note). Add the vanilla and 1 tablespoon of the cold water and fold the dough together using a rubber spatula. Continue to add the water, 1 tablespoon at a time, until the dough just holds together.

DIVIDE the dough in half and form it into two discs, dusting it with a bit of flour if it sticks when you work with it. Wrap each disc in plastic wrap and refrigerate them for at least 2 hours before using or up to 3 days. Wrapped well, they can be frozen for up to 3 months.

Cook's Note: We learned to make piecrust by hand, but you can also use a food processor if you prefer!

Mini Vegan Sweet Potato Pies

JAKE: When I was fifteen years old, Jazz and I started a pie business; we sold our pies in local SoCal health food grocery stores. We made five-inch mini pies, and they were vegan, which at the time was unusual. (We were sweetening them with honey until a customer reminded us that honey is an animal product. Those darn vegans and their rules!) Anyway, soon after launching a business, Jazz ditched me to move back to New York and study at NYU. Jurnee took her place and was the new Smollett sister pie baker, and we delivered hundreds of mini pies a week to local stores (without the honey of course). This sweet potato pie has very few ingredients, but you'll see how unnecessary the other stuff is. Pair this with vanilla ice cream, or dairy-free coconut "ice cream" for a vegan option.   MAKES SIX 5-INCH PIES

---

6 medium yams, peeled (see Note)

1 cup packed brown sugar

1 teaspoon pure vanilla extract

1½ teaspoons ground cinnamon

½ teaspoon ground nutmeg

1 recipe Perfect Piecrust (page 230)

Flour, for rolling out the dough

SPECIAL EQUIPMENT: six 5-inch pie tins

BRING a large pot of water to a boil and cook the yams for about an hour, or until soft. Drain the yams and put them directly into a food processor to puree (or use a handheld mixer). It's best to puree the yams when they are still hot because they will mash easier. When the yams are a smooth consistency, place them in a large bowl and mix in the brown sugar, vanilla, cinnamon, and nutmeg. Stir to make sure all the ingredients are married to the sweet potatoes. Set aside.

PREHEAT the oven to 375°F.

LIGHTLY dust a clean work surface and your hands with flour, then roll out the pie dough. Use a paring knife to cut rounds that are just a little bigger than the diameter of the pie tins. Transfer the dough rounds to the tins, pressing to adhere to the sides, and use a fork to poke holes in the bottom. Set the tins on a rimmed baking sheet and bake the crusts empty ("blind bake" them) for 5 minutes. This will keep the crusts from getting soggy.

USE a small spoon to divide the filling among the crusts and bake for 20 to 25 minutes, until the filling is firm and caramel-like on top and the crust is golden and flaky. Serve immediately or let cool completely, then wrap in plastic wrap and store at room temperature for up to 5 days.

Note: So, we use yams for our sweet potato pie, as does everyone we know and our family always has for generations. They are actually sweeter and more flavorful than sweet potatoes.

Coconut Cream – Chocolate Mousse

JAZZ: I went to Panama a few years ago with my husband. We ended up on a small island called Isla Taboga doing nothing all day but hanging at the beach; playing with stray dogs; eating chicken, beans, and plantains; and drinking fresh coconut water from green coconuts that were broken open with a machete. Ever since then, the coconut and I have been inseparable. I love how versatile they are; I like using them in my desserts as a binder, flavor enhancer, or dairy replacement. This chocolate mousse is dairy-free, for those who are sensitive to dairy, and it tastes awesome! It's the perfect dessert to serve at a cocktail party, and it gives you reason to make small talk about coconut all night!

MAKES 6 TO 8 SERVINGS

CHOCOLATE MOUSSE

Two 13.5-ounce cans coconut cream, chilled, solid parts only

2 teaspoons pure vanilla extract

5 tablespoons coconut sugar

9 ounces semisweet chocolate, chopped into small pieces

WHIPPED "CREAM"

One 13.5-ounce can coconut cream

1 teaspoon pure vanilla extract

2 teaspoons coconut sugar

CHOCOLATE SHAVINGS

One 4.4-ounce bar semisweet chocolate

CHILL a large metal bowl in the freezer. To make the mousse, scoop the chilled coconut cream solids (discard any liquid) into the cold bowl. Using a hand mixer, combine the coconut cream, vanilla, and sugar. Mix on high for about 1 minute, until evenly combined. (You can also use a stand mixer to do this.) Set aside.

BRING to a boil 2 inches water in a small saucepan. Fit a glass or metal bowl over the pan, making sure the water doesn't touch the bottom of the bowl, and reduce the heat to a simmer. Place the chopped chocolate in the bowl and let it melt, stirring often until smooth. (You can also use a microwave to melt it in a small microwave-safe bowl.) Let

the chocolate stand for a few minutes to cool slightly.

ADD the chocolate to the cream mixture and whip until combined and airy, about 1 minute.

COVER the bowl with plastic wrap and place it in the freezer for 1 hour, or until set. Whip the mixture again with the mixer, cover it again, and refrigerate until ready to serve.

WHILE the mousse is freezing, make the whipped "cream." Combine the coconut cream (if there is liquid in the bottom of the can, use only the solid creamy portion; discard the liquid), vanilla, and sugar in a

medium bowl. Whip with a hand mixer or stand mixer on high for about 1 minute, until combined. Cover and freeze for 35 minutes. Remove it from the freezer, whip the mixture again, cover it, and refrigerate until ready to serve.

CHILL your chosen serving glasses in the freezer for about 7 minutes. Divide the mousse among the glasses and top it with a spoonful of the coconut cream. Using a vegetable peeler, shave chocolate over the glasses, then serve.

Vanilla-Rose Pound Cake

JAZZ: I have always been told that I favor my grandmother on my mother's side in my demeanor and look. I've always felt an odd connection to the beautiful grandmother that I never met; she passed away three years before I was born.

A couple of years ago, I traveled to Galveston, Texas, where my mom was born and where the family lived before they moved to New Orleans. As I stood on the wharf, walked the streets, or sat in the library doing hours of family research, I felt the presence and the spirit of my grandma. The wind blew around me in a special way in that town, as though she were speaking to me. People I met there who knew her said that she had a presence. They referred to her as "Showtime," which I can understand, knowing the women in my family.

I was inspired to create this lovely and fabulous floral pound cake in honor of my trip and my grandma. It has a delicate hint of rosewater and citrus, each of which adds a taste of absolute joy. Be sure to use a good-quality pure rosewater, such as Pure Rose by Royal Sense. You can make these and give them away as gifts to your fam and friends or keep them all and freeze! To the fabulous and colorful women in our family and yours: Hugs!

MAKES 6 MINI LOAVES (4 SERVINGS PER LOAF) AND ENOUGH TOPPING FOR 4 SERVINGS (SEE COOK'S NOTE)

POUND CAKE
½ pound (2 sticks) unsalted butter, at room temperature, plus more for greasing

3 cups unbleached all-purpose flour, plus more for dusting

3 cups castor sugar (superfine cane sugar)

5 eggs

2 teaspoons pure vanilla extract

⅔ cup rosewater

1 teaspoon lemon oil

1 teaspoon salt

½ teaspoon baking soda

¾ cup buttermilk

ROSEWATER GLAZE
2 tablespoons unsalted butter, melted

1 cup confectioners' sugar

2½ tablespoons rosewater

½ teaspoon pure vanilla extract

1 tablespoon fresh orange juice

STRAWBERRY TOPPING
12 fresh strawberries, hulled

¼ cup mango juice

1 tablespoon confectioners' sugar

SPECIAL EQUIPMENT: 6 mini loaf pans

PREHEAT the oven to 350°F. Grease and flour 6 mini loaf pans and place them on one large or two small rimmed baking sheets.

TO make the pound cake, in a large bowl cream the butter and sugar with a hand mixer until smooth and pale in color, about 2 minutes. Add the eggs one at a time and mix until incorporated. Mix in the vanilla and rosewater. The mixture may look slightly curdled, but that's the way it's supposed to be. Stir in the lemon oil.

COMBINE the flour, salt, and baking soda in a medium bowl. Mix the flour mixture into the batter in thirds, alternating with the buttermilk: flour mix, buttermilk, flour mix, buttermilk, flour mix! Mix until completely smooth.

DIVIDE the batter evenly among the six pans. Transfer the baking sheet(s) to the oven and bake for 40 minutes, until a toothpick inserted in the center comes out clean. When cool enough to handle, remove the cakes from the loaf pans and set them on a cooling rack.

TO make the glaze, whisk together the butter, sugar, rosewater, vanilla, and orange juice. Spoon the glaze over the cooled cakes. Let set before serving.

TO make the strawberry topping, bring the strawberries and mango juice to a boil in a small saucepan over medium heat. Reduce the heat to medium-low and simmer until the berries begin to soften and meld into the juice, about 10 minutes. Add the sugar and cook for 5 to 7 minutes, until the liquid has reduced and thickened. Let cool slightly.

SLICE the cakes and serve them with the topping. Spoon the strawberry topping over the cake slices.

Cook's Note: You can get four servings from 1 mini loaf, and the strawberry topping makes enough for 1 loaf. Serve the loaves as desired and share and give any extras as gifts during the holidays! Wrap them in plastic wrap and store them for up to 4 days at room temperature.

Oatmeal–Raisin Cookies

JURNEE: Mommy's classic oatmeal-raisin cookies are unrivaled! There's nothing like coming home to the aroma of fresh oats, cinnamon, and plump raisins baking in the oven. Because they were a favorite among friends and colleagues, Mommy would often bake these in bulk, package them in beautiful little bags, and give them away as thank-you gifts.

MAKES ABOUT 24 COOKIES

5 cups rolled oats
1 teaspoon ground cinnamon
¾ teaspoon baking soda
½ teaspoon sea salt
8 tablespoons (1 stick) salted butter, at
    room temperature

½ cup packed dark brown sugar
⅓ cup honey
2 large eggs
2 cups raisins

PLACE a rack in the center of the oven and preheat the oven to 350°F. Line two baking sheets with parchment paper and set aside.

PULSE 2 cups of the oats in a food processor for 5 minutes, or until the oats are turned into flour. This will yield about 1¾ cups oat flour. Combine the oat flour, cinnamon, baking soda, and salt in a medium bowl.

BEAT together with a hand mixer until smooth the butter, sugar, and honey in a large bowl. Add the eggs and whisk until fully incorporated. Fold the oat flour mixture into the butter mixture, followed by the remaining 3 cups oats and the raisins.

SCOOP ¼ cup cookie dough into your hand, roll it into a ball, place it on a prepared baking sheet, and press it with your palm to flatten it slightly. Repeat with the rest of the dough, leaving at least 1 inch between cookies.

BAKE for 15 minutes, or until the cookies are brown around the edges but still soft in the center. Let the cookies cool for 10 minutes, then serve. Store the cookies in an airtight container at room temperature for up to 1 week.

Caramel-Apple Empanadas

JAKE: I'm gonna be honest—I have an ongoing love affair with fast-food desserts. I was inspired to make my own caramel-apple empanadas because I asked myself a serious question. I said, "Self, how can I bite into a warm, gooey, caramel-filled apple pie and not be inspired to make one of my own?" Here's my version of one of my favorite fast-food desserts. Caramel-apple empanadas, I thank you from the bottom of my heart and stomach.

MAKES 24 EMPANADAS

2 Granny Smith apples, peeled, cored, and cut into ¼-inch dice
½ cup packed light brown sugar
2 tablespoons salted butter
1 tablespoon fresh lemon juice
½ teaspoon pure vanilla extract
1 teaspoon ground cinnamon
¼ teaspoon ground nutmeg
1 tablespoon cornstarch
1 recipe Perfect Piecrust (page 230)
Flour, for rolling out the dough
1 egg, lightly whisked
Sugar, for sprinkling

TO make the filling, combine the apples, brown sugar, butter, lemon juice, vanilla, cinnamon, and nutmeg in a medium high-sided skillet over medium heat. Cook for about 5 minutes, or until the butter and sugar create a caramel sauce. Stir in the cornstarch, bring the mixture to a boil, and cook 3 to 4 minutes, until the caramel thickens; when you stir the mixture, your spoon should leave a trail behind it. Let the mixture cool completely off the heat.

LINE two baking sheets with parchment paper. Remove the dough from the fridge. If the dough is too hard to roll out, let it stand at room temperature for 10 to 15 minutes. Lightly dust a clean work surface and your hands with flour and roll out the first disc of dough to ¼ inch thick. Using a 3½-inch round cutter, cut the dough into circles, placing the circles on a baking sheet as you cut them. Combine the scraps and roll out the dough to make more circles, then repeat with the second dough disc. You want about 12 circles per dough disc.

PREHEAT the oven to 350°F.

PLACE a heaping teaspoon of cooled filling into the center of a round of dough and fold the dough over the filling to create a half-moon shape. Use a fork to seal the edge of the empanada, then use a sharp knife to make a slit in the top for a vent. Repeat to make the remaining empanadas. (Reserve any leftover filling for a dipping sauce.)

BRUSH the tops of the empanadas with the egg and sprinkle them generously with sugar. Bake for 18 to 20 minutes, until the crust is golden brown and the filling begins to bubble out the top of the vent. Let cool completely on the baking sheets, at least 20 minutes, and serve.

Peach Cobbler

JURNEE: As much as Mommy loves to bake, she also loves to give away her baked goods, and friends, family members, and colleagues have always been on the receiving end of her generous baking spirit. My sister, Jazz, and brother Jake had the idea to start a little business called Mommy's Baked Goods. These peach cobblers were our top sellers; they'd fly off the shelf. I'll never forget what it was like to bake a hundred miniature pies in two days. Cooking under that sort of pressure and demand was certainly challenging, but it was rewarding, too. One time near the holidays, when Jake and I were in our commercial kitchen preparing a large order for delivery to the local health food store, we were listening on repeat to a mixtape my then friend (and now husband) Josiah Bell had sent me, to keep us dancing while cooking. Jake and I finally realized we liked eating the pies way more than we enjoyed selling them!

MAKES 8 TO 10 SERVINGS

Four 15-ounce cans peaches in light syrup
1 cup packed dark brown sugar, plus more for sprinkling
1 teaspoon ground cinnamon
½ teaspoon ground nutmeg, plus more for sprinkling

Juice of 1 lemon (about ¼ cup)
1½ teaspoons pure vanilla extract
½ cup cornstarch
1 recipe Perfect Piecrust (page 230)
Flour, for rolling out the dough
1 egg, lightly whisked

PREHEAT the oven to 350°F.

DRAIN the peaches (reserve the liquid) and place them in a medium saucepan. Add the brown sugar, cinnamon, nutmeg, lemon juice, and vanilla. Whisk together in a small bowl 1 cup of the reserved peach liquid and the cornstarch until smooth. Pour the mixture into the saucepan, stir, and bring the peaches and liquid to a boil. Reduce the heat to medium and cook, stirring frequently, until the mixture has thickened, about 5 minutes. Set aside to cool slightly.

LIGHTLY dust a clean work surface with flour, then roll out a disc of dough large enough to fit an 8 × 8-inch baking dish and come up the sides. Lay the dough in the dish, pressing it into the edges of the dish and smoothing it out. Pour the peach filling into the dish.

ROLL out the other dough disc and break it into rough pieces. Top the cobbler with the dough pieces, arranging them rustically. You can overlap them so that you cover all the peach mixture, but you don't need to press the top dough into the dough at the edges of the pan. Brush the top crust with the egg and lightly sprinkle it with more brown sugar and nutmeg.

BAKE for 65 to 70 minutes, until the crust is golden and the filling is bubbling.

Cast-Iron Strawberry-Rhubarb Pie

JAKE: One thing for sure is that I got my love for cast-iron pots and pans from my mom. She literally owns every shape and size of cast iron available. Baking a pie in cast iron adds a signature crust that only a cast-iron-baked pie can achieve. This pie is tart and beautiful with strawberries and rhubarb as the stars and the flaky crust complementing them. This is how I like my pie! **MAKES 6 TO 8 SERVINGS**

---

1 pound frozen rhubarb

2 pounds frozen strawberries

½ cup fresh lemon juice (from 2 large lemons)

1½ cups packed dark brown sugar, more for sprinkling

¼ cup cornstarch

3 teaspoons pure vanilla extract

2 teaspoons ground cinnamon, plus more for sprinkling

1 recipe Perfect Piecrust (page 230)

Flour, for rolling out the dough

1 egg, lightly whisked

PREHEAT the oven to 350°F.

BRING to a boil the rhubarb, strawberries, lemon juice, and brown sugar in a large saucepan, then reduce the heat to medium. Whisk together the cornstarch and ¼ cup water in a small bowl. Add this slurry to the pan, plus the vanilla and cinnamon. Stir and cook for 20 minutes, or until the rhubarb breaks down and the strawberries become soft. The mixture should look like a chunky jam.

LIGHTLY dust a clean work surface with flour, then roll out 1 dough disc into a round that will fit a 10-inch cast-iron skillet and go up the sides. Lay the dough in the pan and press it gently into the edges. Add the filling to the pan.

ROLL out the second dough disc and cut it into 1-inch strips. Lay the strips across the top of the pie horizontally, about an inch apart, then layer more strips on top vertically across the pie. Press the edges to seal. Brush the lattice with egg wash and sprinkle it with more brown sugar and cinnamon.

BAKE for about 45 minutes, or until the lattice is golden and the filling is bubbling. Let cool for a few minutes before serving.

Brown Sugar Doughnuts

JAZZ: One of the sweetest things about becoming a mom has been seeing a new world through my baby's eyes. Everything is a wonder for her: the first raindrops she heard, her first steps, and the first time she ate a doughnut! For me, baking isn't just about the finished product; it's about the process as well. The process is particularly fun because Nylah, my now three-year-old daughter, is so ecstatic about helping me in the kitchen. She *loves* pouring, stirring, and of course, tasting!

When something yummy comes out of the oven, she usually exclaims with pride, "I made dat!" I say, "Yes, you did. Good job, baby, it looks so yummy." And she says, "Thank do." I don't mind her taking all the credit because she's the sweetest thing ever and I love her to pieces!

(By the way, these doughnuts are baked rather than fried, which means they're practically guilt-free, right?!)

MAKES 12 SERVINGS

DOUGHNUTS
Baking spray
8 tablespoons (1 stick) unsalted butter
1 cup packed light brown sugar
1 large egg
2½ cups unbleached all-purpose flour
1 teaspoon baking powder
1 teaspoon sea salt
1 teaspoon ground cinnamon

½ teaspoon baking soda
1 cup buttermilk

TOPPING
2 cups confectioners' sugar
¼ cup honey
½ cup packed light brown sugar
1 tablespoon ground cinnamon

SPECIAL EQUIPMENT: two 6-well doughnut pans, pastry bag (or zip-top bag)

PREHEAT the oven to 350°F. Lightly grease two 6-well doughnut pans with baking spray.

MELT the butter in a large microwave-safe bowl in the microwave on high, about 1 minute. Whisk in the sugar until completely combined, then whisk in the egg.

WHISK together the flour, baking powder, salt, cinnamon, and baking soda in a medium bowl. Fold half the flour mixture into the sugar mixture with a rubber spatula and combine completely. Stir in the buttermilk until smooth, then fold in the remaining flour mixture.

SCRAPE the doughnut batter into a pastry bag, snip the tip, and evenly pipe the batter into the doughnut molds. Bake for 15 minutes, or until the doughnuts turn a light golden brown and a toothpick inserted

comes out clean. Let the doughnuts cool for 10 minutes in the pan, then remove them to a cooling rack for glazing.

TO make the glaze, whisk together in a medium bowl the confectioners' sugar, honey, and ¼ cup water until smooth. Whisk together the brown sugar and cinnamon in a small bowl. Set aside.

DIP each doughnut in the glaze on both sides, then immediately dip one side of each into the cinnamon-sugar mixture, and serve. Store the doughnuts in an airtight container at room temperature for up to 3 days.

Uncle Jojo passing on his doughnut obsession.

Apple-Pear-Date Pie

JAZZ: This light and tart pie, which is a twist on the traditional apple pie, will surprise and delight you. I sometimes like to experiment with different ways of sweetening my desserts, and this pie came about because my daughter, Nylah, and I both love dates. The sweetness of a date is like chewing on a piece of sugarcane. But dates are also packed with a ton of nutrients, so it's a great sugar substitute!

MAKES ONE 9-INCH PIE, TO SERVE 6 TO 8 PEOPLE

---

12 Medjool dates, pitted and roughly chopped

2 Granny Smith apples, peeled, cored, and thinly sliced

2 Jonagold apples, peeled, cored, and thinly sliced

Juice from 1 lemon (about ¼ cup)

1 teaspoon pure vanilla extract

1 teaspoon ground cinnamon

3 pinches ground nutmeg

2 tablespoons unbleached all-purpose flour, plus more for rolling out the dough

2 Anjou pears, peeled, cored, and thinly sliced

1 recipe Perfect Piecrust (page 230) or 2 frozen store-bought piecrusts, thawed

1 egg, lightly whisked

PREHEAT the oven to 350°F.

PUREE the dates and 6 tablespoons water in a food processor until completely smooth. Be sure to scrape down the bowl so all pieces are incorporated.

COMBINE the date puree and apples in a medium saucepan. Stir to coat the apples, then add the lemon juice, vanilla, cinnamon, and nutmeg and mix until combined. Mix together in a small bowl the flour and ¼ cup water until smooth, then stir this into the apple-date mixture. Cook over medium heat for about 7 minutes, stirring occasionally, until the mixture has thickened and the apples are easy to pierce with a fork. Remove from the heat and fold in the pears. Let the mixture cool slightly.

LIGHTLY dust a clean work surface and your hands with flour, then roll out a dough disc to fit a 9-inch pan and drape it over the pan. If you're using a frozen crust, make sure it is still cold to the touch before adding the pie filling. Pour the mixture into the piecrust.

ROLL out the second dough disc and cut it into 1-inch strips. (If you're using a refrigerated piecrust, remove it from the tin to a clean work surface. Use a rolling pin to flatten it out evenly, then use a knife or pizza cutter to cut 1-inch-wide strips for the lattice.) Lay the strips across the top of the pie horizontally, about an inch apart, then layer more strips on top vertically across the pie. Press the edges to seal. Brush the lattice with egg wash.

SET the pie on a baking sheet and bake it for 45 minutes, or until the lattice is golden and the filling is bubbling. Let cool for a few minutes before serving. Enjoy!

Dutch Flourless Triple-Chocolate Cake

JAZZ: While living and studying in Amsterdam one summer, I sat at a café one night and drank fresh mint tea and ate chocolate cake. The cake was flourless, but it wasn't a molten cake. This was right before flourless cake became popular in the States, so it was new to me. It was the best chocolate cake I'd ever had, and this is coming from a self-admitted chocoholic! It was dark and rich and so very moist and gooey that it was absolutely irresistible.

I never forgot that cake, and as I got more into baking, I decided to create my own version. Hope you fall head over heels in love with this decadent chocolate dessert the way that I have. Wishing you more love and chocolate!

MAKES ONE 9-INCH CAKE, TO SERVE 8 TO 10

½ pound (2 sticks) plus 1 tablespoon
    unsalted butter, at room temperature

¾ cup plus 1 tablespoon Dutch-
    processed cocoa

1 cup bittersweet chocolate chips

1 cup granulated sugar

5 eggs

1 teaspoon ground cinnamon

1 teaspoon pure vanilla extract

¼ teaspoon sea salt

Confectioners' sugar, for serving

Edible flowers, for serving

PREHEAT the oven to 350°F. Grease the bottom and sides of a 9-inch cake pan with ½ tablespoon of the butter. Cut a piece of parchment to fit the bottom of the pan, lay it in the pan, and grease the top and sides of the parchment with another ½ tablespoon of the butter. Dust the bottom and sides with 1 tablespoon of the cocoa and tap out any excess.

PLACE the remaining ½ pound (2 sticks) butter and the chocolate chips in a medium microwave-safe bowl and microwave on high for 1 minute, until melted. Remove and stir until completely combined. Whisk in the granulated sugar, eggs, cinnamon, vanilla, and salt until completely combined. Then whisk in the remaining ¾ cup cocoa and stir until smooth.

POUR the batter into the prepared cake pan and bake for 25 minutes, or until a toothpick inserted into the center comes out clean. Let the cake cool 10 minutes, then remove it from the cake pan by inverting it onto a tray. Carefully flip the cake right side up and dust with confectioners' sugar before serving. The cake is best served immediately but may be stored in an airtight container at room temperature for up to 2 days.

Coconut Macaroons

JURNEE: I will confess now—I am a certified cookie monster! There's no hope for me. This special little cookie has always been one of my favorites. I love macaroons, not to be confused with French macarons. These cookies became a staple during Jewish holidays because they are naturally without flour or leavening. I think we may rival Manischewitz with our version. I can't describe the joy it gives me to bake these cookies with my niece Nylah. She gets to stir the ingredients in and I get to watch her enjoy the wonders of baking! Shepherd them young!

MAKES ABOUT 25 MACAROONS

---

14 ounces sweetened flaked coconut
   (about 5 cups packed coconut)
1 cup sugar
2 teaspoons pure vanilla extract

1 teaspoon cream of tartar
½ teaspoon sea salt
2 large egg whites

PLACE a rack in the center of the oven and preheat the oven to 275°F. Line two baking sheets with parchment paper and set aside.

COMBINE the coconut, sugar, vanilla, cream of tartar, and salt in a medium bowl. Add the egg whites and mix until completely incorporated. Scoop out 1 heaping tablespoon of the mixture, roll it into a ball in your hands, and place the macaroon on a prepared baking sheet. Continue to form macaroons, evenly dividing them between the two baking sheets and spacing them 1 inch apart, until you've used all the mixture.

BAKE for 45 minutes, rotating the pans halfway through cooking. The macaroons are done when the bottom edges and very tops are golden brown. Let cool for 15 minutes before serving. Store in an airtight container at room temperature for up to 5 days.

SPECIAL FEAST
menus

You don't need us to give you a reason to feast, but here are a few sample menus
you may want to use as inspiration for your gatherings and holidays!

VALENTINE'S DAY
Linguine Vongole 48
Dutch Flourless Triple-
Chocolate Cake 251
Honey-Vanilla Ice Cream 229

SPRING GATHERING
Mini Croque-Monsieurs 169
Spicy Fish Cakes 165
Jewish Deli Deviled Eggs 213
Vanilla-Rose Pound Cake 237
Sweet and Salty
Mixed Nuts 184

FOURTH OF JULY
Finger-Licking BBQ Bacon
Cheeseburger 172
Dill Potato Salad 157
BlaVaMato Salad 117
Drunken Grilled Peaches
with Vanilla and Lemon
Mascarpone 224
Caramel-Apple
Empanadas 240
1980s Vintage Root Beer
Float 73

LABOR DAY PICNIC
Ginger-Spiced Applesauce 192
Jake's Naked Fried Wings 99
Asparagus and Mozzarella
Pasta Salad 140
Kale Caesar Salad 113
Lemon-Lavender
Cupcakes 227

THANKSGIVING
Stuffed Cornish Hens 2
Smoked Cheddar and Creole
Mac-n-Cheese 127
Pancetta-Pomegranate
Brussels Sprouts 130
Creamed Spinach 148
Mini Vegan Sweet
Potato Pies 233
Peach Cobbler 243

CHRISTMAS
Mom's Pot Roast 12
Cheesy Herb Manicotti
Casserole 54
Red Beans with Ham
Hocks 98
Family Collard Greens 136
Cast-Iron Strawberry-
Rhubarb Pie 244
Oatmeal-Raisin Cookies 239

CHANUKAH
Homemade Potato Chips and
Caramelized Onion Dip 186
Brown Butter Lamb Chops 6
Potato Latkes 134
Cheesy Broccoli 153
Coconut Macaroons 252
Matzo Bark 189

NEW YEAR'S DAY
Butter Lettuce Apple Crisp
Salad 114
Pork Tenderloin with
Apricot Dipping Sauce 79
Garlic-Mushroom Quinoa 147
Spicy West African Black-
Eyed Peas 135
Jalapeño-Bacon-Cheddar
Corn Bread 128
Coconut Cream–Chocolate
Mousse 234

UNIVERSAL CONVERSION CHART

OVEN TEMPERATURE EQUIVALENTS

250°F = 120°C

275°F = 135°C

300°F = 150°C

325°F = 160°C

350°F = 180°C

375°F = 190°C

400°F = 200°C

425°F = 220°C

450°F = 230°C

475°F = 240°C

500°F = 260°C

MEASUREMENT EQUIVALENTS

Measurements should always be level unless directed otherwise.

⅛ teaspoon = 0.5 mL

¼ teaspoon = 1 mL

½ teaspoon = 2 mL

1 teaspoon = 5 mL

1 tablespoon = 3 teaspoons = ½ fluid ounce = 15 mL

2 tablespoons = ⅛ cup = 1 fluid ounce = 30 mL

4 tablespoons = ¼ cup = 2 fluid ounces = 60 mL

5⅓ tablespoons = ⅓ cup = 3 fluid ounces = 80 mL

8 tablespoons = ½ cup = 4 fluid ounces = 120 mL

10⅔ tablespoons = ⅔ cup = 5 fluid ounces = 160 mL

12 tablespoons = ¾ cup = 6 fluid ounces = 180 mL

16 tablespoons = 1 cup = 8 fluid ounces = 240 mL

ACKNOWLEDGMENTS

A very special thank-you to Mommy for building the beautiful table on the front cover, we love you to the moon and back.

Thank you to our brothers Jojo and Jocqui for your love and inspiration. Thanks for letting us pull you into this process and for taking time off work at your real jobs to come and play with us.

To everyone in our tribe who supported us through this process and let us throw you into photos: Alex Moran-Smollett, Josiah Bell, Deanna Morgan, Libby and Frankie Jeffries, Kishaya and Bailey Perry, the Jacksons, and Hydeia Broadbent. Our honorary taste-tester, Grace Gibson, who ate tons of food for us. Thank you all for cheering us on, supporting us, and lifting us up always.

Thank you to all of our family and friends who dance, love, and celebrate with us. Thank you for all that you bring to our lives. We could not have done any of this without each of you. Love you all!

Thank you, Cassie Jones, for your keen and creative eye and your thoughtful collaboration. Thank you for lingering on the phone answering a million questions, and for your diligence in helping us make this book the best it could be.

To our agent, Eve Attermann at WME—thank you for your endless support and vision, and for going on this ride with us from the start.

Thank you also to Darrell Miller and Alicia Everett for everything.

To Kara Zauberman, for all of your hard work and dedication to this project.

To Renata De Oliveira, for designing such a beautiful book.

To everyone on the HarperCollins and William Morrow team, but especially Liate Stehlik, Lynn Grady, Anwesha Basu, Tavia Kowalchuk, Shelby Peak, Mumtaz Mustafa, and Anna Brower. We are forever grateful to you all.

Thank you to our culinary team, Ali Clarke, Katie Allen, Hannah Canvasser, and Justin Dega, for your hard work and dedication to this project.

Thank you, Ray Kachatorian, for your artistic eye, for giving us such beautiful photography, and for always saying, "Sure, let's try it!"

Thank you, Jennifer Barguiarena, for executing the vision for the book's photo styling with endless grace. Thank you to our tireless assistants and beauty team, Chloe Flowers, Delaney Hewitt, Taylor Beverly, Autumn Moultry, and Nil Muir. To Ashlee Margolis and Jessica Nagel at the A-List Showroom in Los Angeles. We are forever grateful!

INDEX

Page numbers in *italics* indicate photos

HarperCollins books may be purchased for educational, business, or sales promotional use. For information, please email the Special Markets Department at SPsales@harpercollins.com.

FIRST EDITION

Designed by Renata De Oliveira
Photography by Ray Kachatorian
Family photographs courtesy of the Smollett family

Library of Congress Cataloging-in-Publication Data has been applied for.

ISBN 978-0-06-269395-2

18 19 20 21 22   QDG   10 9 8 7 6 5 4 3 2 1